Wall Street Values

Wall Street Values chronicles the transformation of Wall Street's business model from serving clients to proprietary trading and explains how this shift undermined the ethical foundations of the modern financial industry. Michael A. Santoro and Ronald J. Strauss argue that postmillennial Wall Street is not only "too big to fail" but also a threat to the economy even when it succeeds. They describe how, more than a year before the government acknowledged the financial crisis, Wall Street icon Goldman Sachs saved itself by misleading its clients and impeding the information flow needed for the efficient functioning of free markets, thereby prolonging the mortgage bubble and adding to the financial and human cost of the crisis.

Santoro and Strauss make a compelling case for vigorous government enforcement of the Dodd-Frank Act in the face of Wall Street's opposition. Effective government regulation is not enough; economic prosperity will be sustainable only if Wall Street professionals themselves begin an urgently needed conversation about their values and business ethics.

Michael A. Santoro is a professor of management and global business at Rutgers Business School in New Jersey, where he has taught since 1996. Among Professor Santoro's books is *Ethics and the Pharmaceutical Industry* (Cambridge University Press, 2005, co-edited with Thomas M. Gorrie).

Ronald J. Strauss is an assistant professor at the Montclair State University School of Business and has more than twenty-five years of experience in the financial services industry.

Wall Street Values: Business Ethics and the Global Financial Crisis

❖

Michael A. Santoro
Rutgers Business School, New Jersey

Ronald J. Strauss
Montclair State University, New Jersey

 CAMBRIDGE UNIVERSITY PRESS

CAMBRIDGE UNIVERSITY PRESS
Cambridge, New York, Melbourne, Madrid, Cape Town,
Singapore, São Paulo, Delhi, Mexico City

Cambridge University Press
32 Avenue of the Americas, New York, NY 10013-2473, USA

www.cambridge.org
Information on this title: www.cambridge.org/9781107017351

© Michael A. Santoro and Ronald J. Strauss 2013

First published 2013

Printed in the United States of America

A catalog record for this publication is available from the British Library.

Library of Congress Cataloging in Publication data
Santoro, Michael A.
  Wall Street values : business ethics and the global financial crisis / Michael
A. Santoro, Ronald J. Strauss.
    p. cm.
  Includes bibliographical references and index.
  ISBN 978-1-107-01735-1 (hardback)
  1. Financial institutions – Moral and ethical aspects – United
States. 2. Securities industry – Moral and ethical aspects – United
States. 3. Business ethics – United States. 4. Financial crises – United
States. I. Strauss, Ronald J., 1955– II. Title.
  HG181.S265 2012
  174′.4–dc23   2012024349

ISBN 978-1-107-01735-1 Hardback

Cambridge University Press has no responsibility for the persistence or
accuracy of URLs for external or third-party Internet Web sites referred to in
this publication and does not guarantee that any content on such Web sites is,
or will remain, accurate or appropriate.

Contents

Preface   *page* vii

Acknowledgments   xiii

I   Background and Theoretical Framework

1 A Financial, Governmental, and
       Moral Crisis   3

2 Does Wall Street Have Any Responsibility
       to Society? Wall Street and Economic
       Prosperity   27

**II Wall Street Business Model, Regulation,
     and Values in Transition**

3 The Gathering Storm: Government Missteps
       and Inattentiveness Contribute to the
       Financial Crisis   61

Contents

4 From Financial Services to Proprietary
Trading: The Transformation of Wall
Street's Business Model   90

5 Secrets and Lies: Goldman Sachs and the
Death of the Honest Broker   114

**III Policy Recommendations and
Sustainable Values for Wall Street
in the Twenty-First Century**

6 Wall Street Regulation for the Twenty-First
Century   155

7 Wall Street Values for the Twenty-First
Century   178

Notes   205

Index   223

Preface

More than four years after the financial crisis that erupted in September 2008, there has been no dearth of books analyzing its origins. Numerous government hearings, documentary films, journalistic investigations, and a national independent commission report have all added to our understanding of the crisis. Certainly a reader might reasonably question the purpose of a new book on the subject. Our simple answer is that the financial crisis was fundamentally a crisis of business ethics rooted in almost three decades of moral, financial, and institutional transformation on Wall Street. Indeed, the most important finding of *Wall Street Values* is that business ethics and values matter, and that no amount of structural reform and government regulation will ensure the stability of the global financial system unless the ethical practices and values of Wall Street professionals are aligned with market efficiency and the public welfare. In this book we detail when and how Wall Street's business model and values diverged from the public interest, and we offer a roadmap for realignment.

At the same time that we seek to avoid the Charybdis of redundancy, we are mindful too of the Scylla of obsolescence. As *Wall Street Values* goes to press, each week brings fresh news of Wall Street's ineptitude and malfeasance – the botched Facebook offering by a once top-tier investment bank, a "London Whale" losing billions of dollars in unsupervised trading bets for a global bank renowned for its risk management prowess, and a financial firm entrusted with executing market transactions for customers big and small losing nearly half a billion dollars in one morning because of a software glitch that kept automatically trading without any human control. A reader might reasonably question the point of a book written before these developments fully unfold. Again our answer returns to the primacy of ethics, particularly in a time of change and turmoil. Two and a half millennia ago, Confucius, writing at a time of great transformation and uncertainty in ancient China, compared virtue to the North Star, remaining in its place while all the other stars moved about it. So too we believe that focusing on the ethical roots of the financial crisis elucidates how our financial institutions can operate in a manner that nurtures both profits and social prosperity.

Preface

Just as after the stockmarket crash of 1929 and the subsequent sea change in government regulation of the securities industry Wall Street reinvented itself by focusing on fidelity and service to customers and clients, we believe there is an opportunity today for financial institutions to evolve to a more economically sustainable and socially beneficial business model. This process has already begun. Game-changing reforms, most notably the Dodd-Frank Act, are slowly reawakening and reinvigorating long dormant and outflanked regulatory institutions. The financial industry itself is fitfully undergoing dramatic transformation and reinvention as established institutions try to protect their customary turf and new players endeavor to edge in to prominence. Much more can and needs to be done.

We hope *Wall Street Values* will be of interest to different kinds of readers – concerned citizens, legislators, and regulators, as well as academics and journalists – collectively striving to understand the lessons of the financial crisis for our future. We are also hopeful that *Wall Street Values* will resonate with a global audience. The 2008 financial crisis originated when U.S. financial institutions stimulated a bubble in the U.S. mortgage market. The effects and lessons of the crisis are, however, global. The term "Wall Street" encompasses a global industry, not merely an address in downtown Manhattan. The capital markets are global; the financial system is global. The activities associated with Wall Street – raising capital, originating securities, advising on mergers and acquisitions, trading, brokerage and investment advising – are performed around the clock, across the United States in St. Louis, Chicago, San Francisco, and Dallas, and around the world in Toronto, London, Frankfurt, Paris, Milan, and Tokyo. Moreover, Dubai, Hong Kong, Shanghai, Mumbai, Singapore, and São Paulo, to name but the most obvious, have also emerged as leading financial hubs. Hence, while the great majority of our analysis concerns U.S.-based financial firms and developments in U.S. government regulation, we believe that shrewd observers throughout the world well understand that they have a stake in understanding the ethical roots of the 2008 financial crisis, if only to ensure that they not repeat America's mistakes.

We hope especially that *Wall Street Values* will engage the ingenuity and imagination of financial professionals at all levels of management from the boardroom to the trading floor. Much of what we write about the financial industry is highly critical, but our intention is to engage with industry leaders to initiate a much-needed dialogue about the role of ethics and values as well as the economic and social relationship of Wall Street to Main Street. In the wake of the financial crisis, public opinion about

Preface

Wall Street is at an all-time low. In September 2011, the Occupy Wall Street movement tapped into an outpouring of popular discontent. The predominant image is of individuals who are greedy, unethical, and dismissive of the danger they pose to the broader interests of society. Sad to say, there is no shortage of individuals who fit this stereotype. We also know from our research and personal experience working in the business world that there are many thoughtful executives and leaders on Wall Street who want to make a positive social impact at the same time that they pursue the great personal and corporate wealth the financial industry makes possible. We hope *Wall Street Values* can answer many of the questions and concerns accompanying the increased scrutiny of the role of Wall Street in our economy and society, and also help focus reform efforts to channel this discontent into progressive institutional change. We strongly believe that our collective economic prosperity and our social cohesion will in the future depend on the courage and ability of Wall Street leaders to provide moral leadership. We invite them to consider the moral and economic analysis we present in this book and begin a long-overdue dialogue about Wall Street values.

Acknowledgments

We gratefully acknowledge all the help and encouragement we have received from colleagues, friends, and family.

Scott Parris, our editor at Cambridge University Press, gently guided *Wall Street Values* from an idea to a book. We felt fortunate at every stage for Scott's publishing experience, intellectual vision, and rigor. Kristin Purdy, Frances Bajet, and the rest of the Cambridge team worked with skill and professionalism, allowing us to focus our efforts on research and writing. We also want to thank Michael's good friend Mary Child, who helped shape our ideas for *Wall Street Values* at an early critical stage.

We especially want to thank two friends who contributed both emotional support and intellectual capital. Michael's friend Howard J. Barnet, Jr., took valuable time away from his Wall Street law practice, his family, and his golf game to read and comment on every chapter.

Acknowledgments

Ron's life-long friend Dr. Steven G. Friedman took time away from his medical practice and family life to provide valuable critique of several chapters. Their expertise and passion for the subject made this a better book. Their friendship made the journey more fun.

We are grateful to our business ethics colleagues at various academic institutions and conferences for engaging and critical anonymous reviews (especially those at Cambridge), public dialogues, and private conversations. In particular, we want to express our appreciation to our colleagues at the Society for Business Ethics Annual Meeting and the Annual Ethics Symposium of the American Accounting Association.

Wayne Eastman, Leonard Goodman, Miklos Vasarhelyi, and James Gathii provided helpful comments and criticisms of drafts at various stages. Nancy DiTomaso, Ann Buchholtz, and Dan Stubbs have been strong and effective advocates for business ethics research and teaching at Rutgers Business School. Akiko Shigemoto was always at the ready to perform research and contribute. We are also grateful to Dan Palmon for our joint work on executive compensation in the immediate aftermath of the financial crisis. As Ron made the transition from doctoral candidate to professor, his colleagues in the Accounting Department at Montclair State, particularly Frank Aquilino, James Di Gabriele,

Acknowledgments

Irene Douma and Agatha Jeffers, have fostered a welcoming environment that embraces Ron's research into business and accounting ethics. A grant from the Rutgers Business School Research Resources Committee helped fund our research. The Aresty Center at Rutgers University provided funding for three outstanding undergraduate researchers – Larry Sukernik, Rachel Greenberg, and Rahul Prabhudesai. Our students at Rutgers Business School and Montclair State have patiently endured and helped us clarify our work-in-progress ideas, and the assistance provided by Rutgers department secretary Stephanie Gutierrez has been much appreciated.

A group of Wall Street executives, including several former colleagues, provided illuminating deep background and sobering reality checks about the financial industry. We have honored their sensitive positions by keeping their names anonymous but we are very grateful for their time and insights.

Finally, Ron would like to express his gratitude to his wife Jennifer and son Ben for their understanding and encouragement during the writing of this book. Jennifer has been a cherished partner, always available to edit, comment, and exchange ideas. To Ben, Ron writes: "My hope for this book is that it contributes to a better world for you and your generation."

— ♣ PART ONE ♣ —

Background and Theoretical Framework

CHAPTER ONE

A Financial, Governmental, and Moral Crisis

Introduction

On Monday, September 15, 2008, Lehman Brothers, a prominent investment bank that traces its roots to 1850, declared bankruptcy and thereupon triggered a global financial crisis. Literally overnight, borrowing came to a standstill, and widely held assets could not be converted into cash. The liquidity crunch immediately crippled banks owning substantial amounts of securities linked to subprime mortgages and spread very quickly to every sector of the global economy and all types of debt securities. Unable to sell even normally safe and highly liquid investments, on Tuesday, September 16,

2008, the Primary Reserve Fund, the oldest money market fund in the United States, in an action eerily reminiscent of Depression-era bank runs, shocked the financial community by freezing customer accounts and indefinitely halting withdrawals. Ordinary consumers were thus harshly reminded that there were no safe havens for their savings in this economic storm, adding another layer of uncertainty and instability to the financial markets. Within weeks of the Lehman bankruptcy, the resulting shock to the financial system inflicted severe and long-lasting damages on the economy, throwing tens of millions of people out of work and slowing economic growth. Half a decade later, the global economy still limps along in the aftermath of the financial crisis.

The financial crisis sprang from a precipitous decline in the value of mortgage-related securities. The bursting of the mortgage bubble completely wiped out Lehman's capital base. Other venerable Wall Street institutions including Merrill Lynch and Bear Stearns narrowly averted total collapse through hastily arranged mergers with Bank of America and JPMorgan Chase, respectively. Virtually every major financial institution had massive exposure to the mortgage market relative to its capital base, and even those banks not in danger of imminent collapse suffered staggering losses severely limiting their ability to engage in ordinary consumer lending activities and basic interbank transactions. Because of the financial sector's centrality to capital and credit markets, the U.S. Congress authorized a $700 billion government bailout to prevent further failures and safeguard the financial system from total collapse.

The global financial crisis and the prolonged economic recession that ensued raise complex and vexing questions inextricably melding economics and morality. What are the economic and moral connections between Wall Street and the overall economy? How did we arrive at this point in history where our most powerful financial institutions and the putative engine room of capitalism thwart rather than promote our free markets, our prosperity, and even our social cohesion? What essential elements and systemic features of our financial system make it possible for a very few individuals to amass enormous personal wealth as they help plunge the rest of society into a deep and enduring economic recession, putting millions out of work? What can be done both within the financial community and by governments to repair the fractured relationship between Wall Street and Main Street? These are the economic, ethical, and public policy questions we address in this book.

Financing the Debtor Nation: A Brief Overview of the Origins of the Financial Crisis

The story of how Wall Street firms became "too big to fail" and had to be saved at considerable taxpayer expense has been much chronicled in once esoteric terminology that has become all too colloquial for ordinary citizens. The seeds of the crisis were being sown for years by overleveraged banks and pension funds from Mississippi to Dusseldorf that placed outsized and risky financial bets on the value of collateralized debt obligations (CDOs) packaged and sold by Wall Street firms and based on an unreliable stream of payments by overleveraged American homeowners holding subprime mortgages. CDOs are financial instruments created by Wall Street firms that divide debt instruments into slivers (tranches), each of which is entitled to a precisely defined slice of the future cash flows from the original pool of future payments. The most common debt instruments whose future cash flows were repackaged in this manner were mortgages – loans secured by real property owned by homeowners and investors. The classic CMO, or collateralized mortgage obligation, was created by pooling mortgages that were then repackaged into a wide variety of tranches, each with rights to precisely defined mortgage-backed cash flows. Consequently, each CMO slice had unique risk and return characteristics.

Ironically, the invention of CDOs was one of the most important and socially useful financial innovations of the late twentieth century. It allowed investors to precisely calibrate the mixture of risk and return they wished to assume when investing in debt-based securities. In this sense, CDOs represented an important advance in the efficiency of capital markets. CDOs also offered advantages to homeowners and borrowers by enabling substantial flows of capital into debt markets, thereby making it easier for consumers to access credit to help purchase everything from a car to a house. In 2004, for example, homeownership rates in the United States reached 69.4 percent. (It has since slipped down to 66 percent.) Of course, the flip side of this easy credit has been a spike in consumer debt and a high incidence of personal bankruptcy among overextended consumers – 1.5 million in 2010 alone. The fatal misstep inexorably leading to the financial crisis arose from the proliferation of CMOs based on subprime mortgages of borrowers with high credit risks based on debt payment history, income qualifications, or other actuarially based indicators. Further contributing to the magnitude of Wall Street's financial bet on subprime mortgages was the invention of synthetic CMOs or derivatives. Unlike the classic CMO constructed from real cash flows from real mortgages, derivatives used contracts to mimic the underlying economics of particular slices of actual pools of mortgages. Neither party to the derivative contract actually owned any interest in the underlying mortgages being referenced in the derivative contract. This methodological innovation unleashed exponential growth in the total mortgage-related debt market and dramatically increased systemic risk in the financial markets.

Catalyzing all this was a cavalcade of incompetence, corruption, and fecklessness. Rating agencies such as Standard & Poor's and Moody's assigned investment grades to subprime CMOs, thereby promoting the idea that financial alchemy devised by Wall Street wizards would enable investors to enjoy the high returns normally associated with risky investments with the security normally reserved for more modest financial returns; subprime loan originators such as Countrywide, Washington Mutual, and Ameriquest that cut corners on standards and documentation to feed the pipeline of mortgage-backed securities that Wall Street craved; mismanaged quasi-federal agencies such as Freddie Mac and Fannie Mae, which (utilizing below-market-rate capital made possible by an implicit government guarantee) purchased ever-increasing amounts of subprime mortgages from the originators, thus allowing them to make additional poorly documented and risky loans; mono-line insurers such as AIG, which failed to understand the individual and aggregate of risk they were creating by guaranteeing so many transactions for diverse institutional players in the mortgage markets; and of course the lawyers and accountants who saw, heard, and spoke no evil and who blithely papered over the whole fiasco. It should probably also be said that partial blame must go to some consumers who irresponsibly took out mortgages for amounts they should have known they would not be able to repay, although, to be fair, there were many other consumers who were duped and defrauded by loan originators into taking out loans that were inappropriate for them or contained misleading terms.

Although we do consider these various other actors, our principal focus in this book is on Wall Street, the group of large and powerful financial institutions that orchestrated the financial crisis. We also devote considerable attention to how the government facilitated and exacerbated the financial crisis – first by promulgating regulatory loopholes allowing the market for CMOs and derivatives to grow exponentially and without public oversight, and then by falling asleep at the wheel and being caught completely off guard by the gathering storm. Moreover, as we shall describe in greater detail, the unintended consequences of government policies helped sever the connection between Wall Street profits and free markets that had served the economy well for more than a half-century.

The 99%: Occupy Wall Street and Public Anger over the Bailout

For ordinary citizens, the specter of a $700 billion publicly funded Wall Street bailout was infuriating. Adding insult to injury, many Wall Street executives walked away with huge compensation packages. Even executives in financial firms that declared bankruptcy enriched themselves with outsized cash bonuses as the global economy was thrown into turmoil, and tens of millions of workers around the world ended up out of work. In 2011, that anger spilled over into the streets as Occupy Wall Street protesters set up tents in Zuccotti Park, just steps from the epicenter of capitalism. The group decried economic inequality (hence the rallying cry "we are the 99%") and corporate influence over the government, but its principal eponymous target was Wall Street and the financial services industry. Some have questioned the efficacy and propriety of its direct action tactics. Nonetheless, Occupy Wall Street was emblematic of a broad public disaffection with the financial industry. According to the National Opinion Research Council, from 2006 to

2010, the percent of Americans with a great deal of confidence in banks and financial institutions plummeted 19 percentage points, from 30 percent to an all-time low of 11 percent. Harris Interactive reported that the percent of Americans with confidence in the people running Wall Street reached an all-time low of just 4 percent in February 2009.[1]

The heightened scrutiny of Wall Street revealed a disturbing picture of an overhyped and poorly managed industry whose business model is unhinged not only from the interests of clients and customers but also from the economic realities of the free market. Instead of bringing discipline and sober valuation to the markets, Wall Street recklessly led the orgy of speculation and greed. It created the problems and hid them from public view. Wall Street bankers engineered the Rube Goldberg-like financial instruments that exponentially increased the systemic risks of CMOs. In the years leading up to the financial crisis, Wall Street, the ultimate assessor of value for the rest of the economy, managed to hide its own financial performance flaws from the usually swift and harsh discipline imposed by the free market.

The historical association of the financial industry with Wall Street dates back to the Buttonwood Agreement. On May 17, 1792, twenty-four brokers met under a buttonwood tree in front of 68 Wall Street to found what is now the New York Stock Exchange.[2] However, Wall Street, as we conceive it in this book, is not delineated by a physical place – that half-mile-long cavernous lane running east-west at the lower tip of Manhattan in New York City. Our focus is on the functions essential to capitalism that traditionally have been performed by institutions located on Wall Street, to wit the raising of investment capital, origination of securities, pricing of assets and securities, trading, brokerage and investment advice, market making, and provision of liquidity, as well as the rendering of advice about mergers, acquisitions, and other corporate restructurings. In the United States, many of these functions might also be performed in Chicago, St. Louis, San Francisco, or Dallas, among other places. London, Frankfurt, Milan, and Tokyo each have long and distinguished histories as financial capitals. And today, of course, the capital markets are global and around the clock so that Shanghai, Mumbai, Sao Paulo, and other cities have emerged as important financial hubs. Still, however, the association of Wall Street with the financial industry in the global imagination is a strong one. Moreover, many of the institutions that engineered and were key players in the financial crisis – Goldman Sachs, JPMorgan Chase, Lehman Brothers, Merrill Lynch, and Bear Stearns – originated on Wall Street and, those that survived at least, still have their global corporate headquarters in New York City.

The gap between Wall Street's prosperity and society's overall economic welfare has been widening as a result of the transformation of its business model from a mostly customer orientation with a relatively small proprietary trading component to one in which trading operations have come to dominate its profit structure and, perhaps just as importantly, the attention of the brightest minds in the financial industry. At the same time, a number of developments have increased the sheer scale and scope of Wall Street firms, including, most notably, the repeal of the Glass-Steagall Act, which tore down the wall between investment and commercial banking. These tectonic transformations in the business model and industry configuration of the financial industry have been taking place over three decades. It took the financial crisis, however, to demonstrate that these financial behemoths posed a serious threat to capitalism itself.

The analysis and legal reforms enacted in the aftermath of the financial crisis have focused chiefly on reducing the systemic risks arising when banks become "too big to fail." For example, the Dodd-Frank Act of 2010, the principal legislation enacted to address the financial crisis, was specifically designed according to its preamble to "rein in Wall Street and big bonuses, end bailouts and too big to fail, [and] prevent another financial crisis."[3] The emphasis has been on preventing and containing the systemic consequences of bank failures. Hence, reform efforts to date have sought to decrease leverage, increase capital requirements, and prohibit certain kinds of trading activities by Wall Street firms – most notably principal transactions, where firms buy and sell investments for their own account. We, however, focus on another, equally significant revelation of the financial crisis: Wall Street firms are not only dangerous when they fail; they can do immense damage to the economy even when they succeed. Indeed, as we shall describe, Wall Street launched a financial Armageddon as it made record profits in the years preceding the crisis.

Wall Street today poses a systemic threat to free markets and to capitalism itself. Far from being the impartial engine room of capitalism, Wall Street subtly bends and molds the critical information pathways of the free market to suit its own financial interests. The Wall Street business model and financial agenda have become unhinged from overall economic welfare. The financial system and the economy as a whole need Wall Street to facilitate the accurate valuation of assets and efficient allocation of capital. These functions are crucial to economic expansion, prosperity, and employment growth. However, in the years preceding the financial crisis, instead of facilitating the functioning of free markets, Wall Street prolonged the housing bubble by short-circuiting the flow of accurate market information about the underlying value of mortgage-backed securities. That, in turn, prevented the market from becoming more efficient and quickly detecting the real estate bubble, ultimately raising the financial cost of the bailout and aggravating the human cost of the ensuing economic recession.

Why is it that Wall Street thwarts the free market and poses a threat to capitalism? The problem lies in Wall Street's duality as both an industry and a crucial cog in the larger international economic system. It is structurally and culturally incapable of imposing market discipline on itself with the same ruthlessness that it applies to other industries when performing its essential functions of valuing assets and distributing capital to its most productive uses. Although Wall Street has always had profit motivations, its purely private interests have become much larger and much more disassociated from the interests of its customers and clients. Modern financial firms are financial leviathans that depend heavily on proprietary trading activities for their profits. They are no longer primarily financial services companies. Profits from client and customer relationships are now less significant in comparison to profits from principal transactions, including proprietary trading.

Moreover, when Wall Street is inefficient even for brief periods, the broad negative impacts can be dramatic. There is a rippling effect throughout the entire economy. When its self-interest is at stake, Wall Street distorts the efficient allocation of capital and short-circuits the free flow of information vital to free markets. The long, deep, and socially destabilizing recession that has followed the liquidity crisis triggered by the Lehman Brothers collapse on September 15, 2008, is a testament to the vulnerability of the economy, particularly of workers and entrepreneurs, to Wall Street's lack of market discipline.

The Moral Crisis on Wall Street

Underlying this systemic disconnect between Wall Street profits and social welfare is a deep moral void within the caverns of Wall Street. Public perception of the personal moral values and ethics of Wall Street executives is at historic lows. Only 26 percent of Americans in an April 2011 Harris poll thought the people working on Wall Street were "as honest and moral as other people," as compared to 51 percent in 1997. In the same poll, 67 percent thought "most people on Wall Street would be willing to break the law if they believed they could make a lot of money and get away with it."[4]

A Financial, Governmental, and Moral Crisis

The contemporary Wall Street era can be character-ized, perhaps even defined, by the shift that occurred when financial firms began conceiving of their busi-ness not as customer dependent, but rather as a series of transactions with third parties who came to be known as counterparties. Indeed, the very proliferation of the term "counterparty" into the Wall Street vernacular signals a radical disengagement from an interest in, or depen-dency on, ongoing relationships with people and institu-tions who used to be called clients and customers in the days when investment banking, advice on mergers and acquisitions, brokerage, private client financial advice, and other customer-focused financial services consti-tuted the focus of large financial institutions. In the minds of Wall Street firms, counterparties exist to fulfill the firm's profit ambitions, ambitions that have become increasingly short term and disconnected from the pros-perity and sustainability of the general economy.

It would have been abhorrent for their professional counterparts of yesteryear to deliberately harm custom-ers and clients. The modern Wall Street executive, how-ever, seems morally untroubled even when products such as derivatives, swaps, and other sophisticated financial instruments sold to counterparties are virtually assured to result in losses for those counterparties. Lloyd Blankfein, CEO of Goldman Sachs, captured the essence of the new

Wall Street when he remarked, "We didn't have the word 'client' or 'customer' ... We had counterparties – and that's because we didn't know how to spell the word 'adversary.'"[5] Michael Lewis reports that Morgan Stanley executive Howie Hubler, according to one of several traders closest to him, "thought the customer business was stupid.... Hubler could make hundreds of millions facilitating the idiocy of Morgan Stanley's customers. He could make billions by using the firm's capital to bet against them."[6] One problem with this brave new world of "us versus them" is that no set of ethical principles and internal constraints has emerged to replace the older values that existed when Wall Street profits depended on providing financial services to customers. Wall Street today is morally adrift from its traditional values and a danger to itself and to all with whom it comes into contact in the broader economy. The infamous Goldman Sachs Abacus case (detailed in Chapter five) became an iconic and transformational watershed of Wall Street Values; it was shocking to learn that Goldman Sachs was deliberately selling to its customers a financial instrument that the firm had designed to become worthless. However, despite paying $550 million to settle with the Securities and Exchange Commission (SEC), Goldman itself – and indeed many other Wall Street professionals – steadfastly maintained that the firm had done nothing wrong.

A Financial, Governmental, and Moral Crisis

There is more at stake in the separation of interests between Wall Street firms and their customers than simply the legal and moral duties firms might owe to their customers. The investment banking–client relationships and the broker-customer relationships traditionally fostered on Wall Street were crucial conduits for the free flow of information necessary for the healthy functioning of free markets. When those relationships turned adversarial, the flow of market information became sclerotic and distorted. Inevitably, the financial markets as a whole ceased to function at optimal efficiency.

The financial crisis was fundamentally a crisis of ethics and values. Although we acknowledge the indispensable role of government and regulation, we believe that no amount of government regulation can succeed where the moral core is corrupt. Our emphasis on Wall Street Values comes from our belief that an essential component of the solution to the growing gap between the interests of the financial community and the interest of society must come from the private sector. Unless Wall Street itself formulates a coherent moral response to the crisis, no amount of regulatory oversight will prevent another, potentially more destabilizing, crisis from occurring. The sustainability of capital markets ultimately depends on the moral underpinnings of the people and institutions that drive financial markets.

— ❖ 19 ❖ —

Without a radical transformation of ethics and values in the financial community, the system as a whole is fundamentally unsustainable. It is thus in the interest of financial professionals themselves to support and lead their own moral instauration and a recasting of Wall Street Values.

Although as business ethicists we are hopeful that Wall Street will understand the need to consider questions about values and ethics, we believe that government also has an indispensible role in protecting the public interest. To borrow one of the more memorable concepts from the nuclear age, governments should "trust but verify" when it comes to markets. We appreciate the power of free markets to generate value that can benefit all of society, but we also believe governments must monitor financial markets to verify that they are indeed competitive and to enforce basic ground rules of information flow and other essentials of economic efficiency. The less effort Wall Street undertakes to clean up its own house, the more government will have to step in and do the job. The modern state, however, has limited power to protect the public interest, particularly in a technologically innovative context in which capital has become so large, so concentrated, and so global. At the end of the day, no amount of government regulation will keep us safe from future economic crises unless

Wall Street executives begin to think and act in a more socially responsible manner.

It is not an option to return to the halcyon days of mid-twentieth-century Wall Street when the industry and society prospered together. New ethical principles must emerge in the twenty-first century to sustain the integrity and social responsibility of complex modern financial institutions. How did Wall Street Values stray so far from a healthy and sustainable connection with the public interest? What Wall Street Values are required to sustain the financial industry and the economy in the twenty-first century? We believe that Wall Street, the City of London, Frankfurt, Tokyo, Shanghai, Dubai, Sao Paolo, and other global financial capitals must adhere to clear and strong ethical precepts for their own financial survival as well as for the benefit of our shared general welfare. Our hope is that this book will help motivate Wall Street to reinvigorate and reinvent its moral code, values, and expectations to bring them up to date with the new and complex business models that are evolving in the second decade of the twenty-first century.

Plan of the Book

We begin our analysis in Chapter two by setting forth a minimalist conception of corporate social responsibility advocated by the iconic economist and free market advocate Milton Friedman. According to this view, the sole social responsibility of business is to increase profits. We apply a minimalist social responsibility standard to the financial industry because Wall Street professionals universally espouse the libertarian, classical economic ethos on which this conception is built. However, we demonstrate that the modern financial industry fails even this minimal test of social responsibility. Moreover, when Wall Street is inefficient and the hard economic rules that underpin the minimalist conception are even temporarily nullified, the negative impacts on the economy can be dramatic. There is a rippling effect throughout the entire economy. Wall Street poses a threat to capitalism because it can distort the efficient allocation of capital and short-circuit the free flow of information vital to free markets. In particular, new businesses and ordinary workers are vulnerable. The long, deep, and socially destabilizing recession that has followed the 2008 financial crisis is a testament to the vulnerability of the economy to Wall Street's lack of market discipline.

In Chapter three, we describe the unintended consequences of government policies further severing the connection between Wall Street profits and free markets. The institutional seeds of the financial crisis came in the form of two massively misaligned and inconsistent ideological and regulatory sea changes in the financial system – an orgy of deregulation, mergers, and capital adventurism that created exponentially larger risks for taxpayers, coupled with a declining and ultimately irrelevant regulatory oversight of the financial markets. There was less and less government involvement until all at once there needed to be more government involvement than could ever before be even imagined. We describe how the post-Depression-era regulatory framework became outmoded in a brave new world of financial derivatives and other investment exotica. Policies implemented by the government dating back to the Clinton era opened the floodgates for massively scaled and risky markets, such as the mortgage-backed security market, eventually leading to the financial crisis. We also reflect on the lessons to be learned from the policy makers, regulators, and academics such as Brooksley Born and Elizabeth Warren that, in the pre-crisis era, expressed ominous, but neglected, warnings about the dangerous levels of systemic risk in the financial system.

In Chapter four, we describe the transformation in Wall Street's business model occurring over roughly the past three decades. We explain how the core values of financial firms shifted from rigorous adherence to customer orientation, trust, and mutuality to one of beggar thy neighbor, where firm profits came from, and often at the expense of, counterparties on the other side of the firm's most profitable transactions. Financial institutions evolved from a mix of customer-focused businesses to turbocharged engines of increasingly complex and abstract financial wealth creation. Perhaps the most obvious telltale sign of this transformation was the massive growth and increasing importance of precisely the kind of proprietary trading, particularly of CMOs and derivatives, that was at the center of the financial crisis. As the traditional customer became detached from Wall Street's traditional core business and values, a maze of derivatives, swaps, and complex financial instruments unimaginable to virtually all the brokers and investment bankers of the twentieth century emerged. We examine the economic and moral consequences when Wall Street firms operate in a manner that is detached from concerns about long-term relations with customers.

Chapter five gets to the heart of the transformation of Wall Street Values. In this chapter, we analyze the complex ethical dimensions of information asymmetry in the financial industry by considering various transactions by Wall Street's most successful, prestigious, and powerful firm in the pre-crisis era – Goldman Sachs. We consider, among other transactions, the infamous Abacus deal, which has become a transformational watershed of Wall Street Values. It was shocking for most people to learn that Goldman Sachs was deliberately packaging a financial instrument that would become worthless and, knowing that it would soon become worthless, was simultaneously selling this product to its customers. We argue that Goldman Sachs and other firms involved in similar transactions did not understand the ethical issues involved because the only values they understood were relevant to an earlier client-driven era, and no coherent principles and bright-line rules have yet emerged to address the ethical challenges of twenty-first-century Wall Street.

In Chapter six, we discuss Wall Street regulation in the twenty-first century. We analyze the central provisions of the Dodd-Frank Act as well as other global reforms. In particular we focus on the Volcker Rule prohibitions on proprietary trading by federally insured banks. We consider whether these measures adequately address the risks that we have identified that Wall Street firms pose to the flow of information in the capital markets and the allocation of capital in the economy.

The book concludes in Chapter seven by building on the work of earlier chapters and offering recommendations to right the ship and ensure the sustainability of financial markets. We propose some areas such as compensation policies and the management of conflict of interest where Wall Street might begin the conversation about business ethics. We argue that the financial crisis was fundamentally a crisis of values, and that unless Wall Street itself formulates a coherent moral response to the crisis, no amount of regulatory oversight will prevent another, potentially more destabilizing, crisis from occurring.

— ❖ CHAPTER TWO ❖ —

Does Wall Street Have Any Responsibility to Society? Wall Street and Economic Prosperity

Introduction: Business and the Social Contract

Do Wall Street firms have any duties to society other than to maximize profits while obeying the law? Many believe that every business owes moral duties extending beyond the bottom line to promote social goals such as human rights, diversity, or the environment.[1] One justification for this expansive view of corporate responsibility is based on the idea of the social contract that Locke, Hobbes, and Rousseau employed to elucidate the moral and political foundations of the state.[2] Just as in political theory society precedes and authorizes the powers of the state, corporate power and wealth are premised on a contract with society. The very existence of a corporation as a "fictitious person" with legal rights and protections for investors – for instance, the "corporate veil" of limited liability protecting shareholders from any personal liability for the debts incurred by the corporation – is made possible by society. The accumulation of wealth by private business is made possible by the fertile ground of social capital and within the stable legal framework and property right protections of civil society. In return, it is reasonable to expect that businesses operate in a manner that benefits society.

This idea of the social contract is a formal moral justification for our intuitive sense that the accumulation of wealth is made possible by communal contributions creating reciprocal social responsibilities for business beyond simply maximizing firm profits. In September 2011, Elizabeth Warren, Harvard Law School professor, chair of the Congressional Oversight panel overseeing the financial industry bailout, and architect of the U.S. Consumer Financial Protection Bureau, expressed this point of view in a direct style that went viral on the Internet and resonated deeply with ordinary citizens:

There is nobody in this country who got rich on their own. Nobody. You built a factory out there – good for you! But I want to be clear.

Does Wall Street Have Any Responsibility to Society?

You moved your goods to market on the roads the rest of us paid for. You hired workers the rest of us paid to educate. You were safe in your factory because of police forces and fire forces that the rest of us paid for. You didn't have to worry that marauding bands would come and seize everything at your factory, and hire someone to protect against this, because of the work the rest of us did. Now look, you built a factory and it turned into something terrific, or a great idea – God bless. Keep a big hunk of it. But part of the underlying social contract is you take a hunk of that and pay forward for the next kid who comes along.[3]

There are widespread expectations that companies operating today, especially those that are publicly held and global, will adhere to this expansive moral standard of corporate social responsibility.[4] Some have pushed the idea of corporate social responsibility even further to suggest that managers should have moral duties to consider the welfare and interests of all "stakeholders" such as employees, contractors, and community residents who are affected by a corporation's activities.[5] As a matter of law, it has been long established that managers have fiduciary duties only to a firm's shareholders.[6] However, a number of states, including California and New York, have passed legislation allowing business enterprises to organize as Benefit Corporations (popularly known as B Corps), thereby freeing managers to take employee, community, and environmental interests into consideration when making decisions.[7]

These expectations about social responsibility have prompted varied constructive responses by corporations. Whether through an affiliated foundation or by direct expenditure, companies donate money, employee time, and other resources to local, national, and international social causes. Hundreds of companies issue some form of annual environmental sustainability and social impact report. Many firms have dozens, and in some cases hundreds, of full-time employees dedicated to social responsibility programs. "Triple bottom line" reporting, adopted by many firms, expands traditional financial reports to include reporting on environmental and social matters. Although there are currently no formal legal mechanisms for enforcing this expansive standard of social responsibility, an informal web of nongovernmental organizations (NGO) and intergovernmental institutions has developed to fill this regulatory void, albeit imperfectly. Perhaps the most notable such effort is the United Nations Global Compact, "a strategic policy initiative for businesses that are committed to aligning their operations and strategies with ten universally accepted principles in the areas of human rights, labour, environment and anti-corruption." The question of how socially minded investors and other interested stakeholders can evaluate and monitor the social responsibility of corporations remains open, as it is still far from settled what factors should be taken into account and how such factors can be measured and publicly reported.

Despite the widespread support for and corporate acceptance of the "expansive" moral standard of corporate responsibility, we do not in this book measure Wall Street by that same rigorous standard applied to the behavior of global companies in other industries. We use instead a less demanding "minimalist" moral standard based on libertarian principles and free-market economic theory. In doing so, we do not intend to endorse the minimalist standard. Our purpose in adopting this weaker moral standard is twofold. First, we believe it would be illuminating to hold Wall Street up to the mirror of the free-market values that it finds most flattering and most in accord with its own libertarian ethos. Second, by demonstrating how it fails to meet even this minimalist economic standard, we are able to highlight the profound negative social impacts of Wall Street's transformation from a vibrant customer-based diversified financial services industry to a steroidal coterie of leveraged trading companies, unhinged from market discipline and posing a danger to social welfare and the very capitalist system it extols.

most productive. There must also be efficient product mix – neither too much nor too little of any one product should be produced. There must be efficient allocation – once final goods are produced there must be a way for trading to take place so that goods wind up in the hands of the people who value each good most highly. Finally, there must be a healthy balance between consumption today and investment for the future.[10]

For Milton Friedman and other free-market advocates the best way for society to achieve these various forms of economic efficiency is by allowing producers to generate whatever they believe will earn them the most profit while consumers are free to buy the products they value the most. The free market, according to this view, is the single most powerful and effective tool for dealing with scarcity and overcoming human poverty. There are exceptions – what economists call market failures – where unfettered, selfishly motivated free-market activity does not result in the greatest overall level of productivity for society. Nevertheless, the central premise of capitalism as an economic and moral system is that for the most part, as the character Gordon Gekko famously declaimed in the movie *Wall Street*, "greed works" (better at least than other, more centrally planned, systems) in creating overall material prosperity.

In addition to being a leading proponent of free-market economics, Friedman was a subtle social and political thinker. He was not so naïve as to think that the goal of overall social economic prosperity assured or trumped the goal of achieving social justice. In fact, in his classic 1962 book *Capitalism and Freedom* he acknowledged the vital role of democratic government in ameliorating the inevitable inequalities that result from free markets.[12] Indeed, the superiority of democratically elected governments over corporate CEOs in shaping social justice agendas was yet another reason in Friedman's view that corporations should stay away from voluntary efforts at social responsibility. That job, Friedman argued, was better left to governments, which, in a democratic society at least, are accountable to their citizens. Without an efficient economy, however, there would not be much wealth to deliberate about in the political arena, and any constraints – even seemingly benign socially beneficial constraints – placed on businesses that kept them from maximizing profits would make the economy less efficient. So it is that Friedman is making a highly moral point when he admonishes that the only social responsibility of business is to increase profits.

Many would argue that Friedman's minimalist economic standard sets the moral bar too low and that we should judge Wall Street by the more expansive standard of corporate social responsibility that we would apply to every other industry. Although we have some sympathy for this point of view, we believe that there is value in examining Wall Street through the minimalist economic and libertarian standard of corporate social responsibility. As we shall see, even seen through this less rigorous standard, Wall Street falls dangerously short of legitimate societal expectations.

Wall Street's Threat to Free Markets

Many Wall Street executives speak grandiloquently about free-market values and libertarian principles. These concepts form the bedrock of Wall Street's ideology and delusional self-conceptions. Addressing the National Press Club in 2002, for example, Henry Paulson intoned, "I come here today as the CEO of Goldman Sachs. But, perhaps even more importantly, I come here as an individual who believes passionately in the strength of our free-market system – a system that generates growth, creates jobs and wealth, rewards initiative, and fosters innovation like no other in the history of the world." Former Merrill Lynch CEO Stan O'Neal's "Letter to Shareholders" in 2006 gushed, "we find ourselves in a remarkable position at the center of global capitalism – the most powerful force for improving lives and creating wealth that the world has ever known." Today after the trillions of dollars of damage and great human toll that Wall Street unleashed all over the world, these words ring hollow. They also serve as a sharp rebuke to Wall Street's failure to meet even the minimalist free-market standard of corporate social responsibility.

How did Wall Street become such a clear and present danger to the free markets to which it is ideologically wedded? The answer stems from its dual nature as an industry where firms seek to maximize profits and a vital cog performing crucial social functions at the epicenter of capitalism. As a profit-seeking industry, Wall Street utilizes capital and labor and produces goods and services. At the same time, Wall Street is also a conduit through which the free market performs many of its essential functions such as valuing assets and distributing capital to its most productive uses. Economic growth, jobs, and technological development all depend on the skill with which Wall Street professionals value assets and facilitate capital investment. So long as the profits made on Wall Street depend on satisfying clients by skillfully providing these vital financial services, Wall Street will be able to meet the minimalist standard of corporate social responsibility. There is no intrinsic reason why the free-market dynamics of Wall

Street would function any differently from other industries – that is, high profits mean it is behaving in socially useful ways. And yet, Wall Street often does not work like that. During the financial crisis, in fact, Wall Street profited handsomely while severely damaging the overall economy.

There are two elements behind Wall Street's unique potential as an industry to inflict systemwide economic damage. First, the likelihood of what might be termed "profit disjunction" (i.e., that profits will become unhinged from the general economic welfare) is greater on Wall Street than it is in other industries. Second, when profit disjunction does occur on Wall Street, the consequences for the financial markets and the economy as a whole can be severe, widespread, and enduring.

Profit disjunction is more likely to occur on Wall Street because, although it constitutes the ultimate mechanism of financial discipline for other companies and industries, it is not as good at imposing self-discipline. We learned from the financial crisis that the supposedly ironclad laws of the free market do not apply as immediately or ruthlessly to Wall Street as they do to other industries. One reason Wall Street seems to violate the basic behavioral constraints of the free market is the moral hazard stemming from being "too big to fail," which incentivizes excessive risk taking by creating an economic context of "heads I win, tails you lose" for large, systemically interconnected financial firms. However, the reasons behind Wall Street's disassociation from free-market economics run much deeper. Wall Street is the "cop on the beat" of the free-market system. Every other industry must come to Wall Street to have its market value determined and possibly to suffer the consequences of economic failure. This is the market discipline of the capitalist system. Create a successful product that consumers want, manage your company effectively and efficiently, and you will enjoy profits as you contribute to society. Create products that no one wants, manage your company ineffectively and inefficiently, and you will lose money and ultimately go out of business. For large capital-intensive businesses, Wall Street is where the drama of that market discipline plays out. Wall Street is cruelly neutral and ruthlessly efficient in dispensing market justice on other industries, but it is a distracted and permissive substitute teacher when it comes to imposing market discipline on itself.

Thoughtful Wall Street professionals understand the crucial role they are entrusted to play in the free markets, although they are less likely to understand and take responsibility for the damage they can inflict when they fail to do this job well. For example, on the eve of the financial crisis, the 2006 Goldman Sachs Annual Report to shareholders blithely proclaimed, "as open markets and global finance transform economies, capital markets will play an increasing vital role in connecting capital to ideas necessary for growth. Goldman Sachs helps allocate capital and manage risk, and through this process fosters entrepreneurship and innovation, drives efficiency and encourages economic reform." These kinds of self-serving statements about Wall Street's promotion of entrepreneurship and innovation rang particularly hollow in the years leading up to the financial crisis when profits from principal transactions and proprietary trading at Wall Street firms came to dwarf profits from traditional investment banking and asset management services for customers. Goldman Sachs itself provides a paradigmatic example. Proprietary trading activities constituted 75 percent of the firm's pretax profits in 2007. Moreover, the profit margins were 42.3 percent in proprietary trading as opposed to 29.8 percent in other areas of the business.[13] Goldman Sachs was hardly unique. Principal transactions in the financial industry as a whole became increasingly dominant as a source of revenues from 2001 to 2007 with the period 2005 to 2007 leading up to the financial crisis being particularly frothy (Figure 2.1).

Does Wall Street Have Any Responsibility to Society?

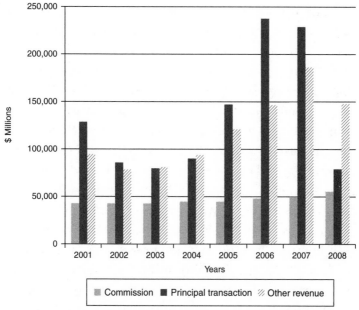

Figure 2.1. *Split of revenues for Wall Street firms, 2001–2008.*
Source: Securities Industry and Financial Markets Association (SIFMA).

This shift was further fueled by the payment of cash bonuses based on principal transactions, which further increased the risk of profit disjunction on Wall Street. Cash compensation paid to Wall Street executives became increasingly dependent upon what turned out to be illusory profits generated by proprietary trading in particular. As the label implies, revenues aggregated into the principal transaction category include trading profits a firm earns as a result of placing its own capital at risk. Financial industry executives pocketed hundreds of millions of dollars in bonuses only to have the profits that those bonuses were based on turn to dust. How did this happen? The trading profits reported by financial firms that formed the basis of bonuses reflect the putative increase in value of the financial assets that a firm owns at the end of any given reporting period. However, these financial assets, including mortgage-backed securities (MBS), have, as we now understand, ongoing economic risks. Wall Street professionals walk away with cash bonuses, but the risk remains on the firm's books. In 2006–2007, nearly $500 million of executive incentives were paid in cash to just the five top executives in seven major financial services firms that failed less than a year later between March 2007 and September 2008 (Table 2.1).

It should be noted that in the wake of the financial crisis Wall Street firms have reformed their bonus compensation practices to take into account the ongoing risks associated with booked trading profits. Many firms have adopted clawback policies that take back bonuses awarded if the executive's division posts a loss in a subsequent reporting period. In February 2012, for example the Swiss-based UBS bank (following a trading scandal

Table 2.1. *Cash incentives for the top 5 senior executives at failed firms*

Firm	2006 cash incentives	2007 cash incentives	Total
AIG	$42,600,000	$32,600,000	$75,200,000
Bear Stearns	$52,300,000	$71,600,000	$123,900,000
Countrywide	$40,100,000	$34,700,000	$74,800,000
Lehman Bros.	$38,100,000	$23,500,000	$61,600,000
Merrill Lynch	$48,800,000	$66,900,000	$115,700,000
Wachovia	$18,000,000	0	$18,000,000
Wash. Mutual	$13,000,000	$11,000,000	$24,000,000
Total	**$252,900,000**	**$240,300,000**	**$493,200,000**

Source: Compiled by authors from company annual reports.

that cost the bank $2.3 billion) took back 50 percent of share-based bonuses awarded in 2011.[14]

Wall Street's Fixation with the Housing Market

When Wall Street, hooked on private trading and a misaligned pay structure, became fixated on MBS, the volatile elements that led to the financial crisis were all in place. Wall Street's profitability became increasingly dependent on proprietary trading; and proprietary trading became increasingly focused on one exceedingly narrow category – securities based upon residential mortgages. This dependency was obsessive and compulsive. While the world outside of Wall Street was experiencing profound globalization of labor markets and trade – with China and other emerging economies rising as manufacturing powers and financial centers – Wall Street executives were pinning their own economic hopes on the sale prices of bungalows in Florida and "McMansions" in Arizona. Wall Street bid the housing bubble up and it bid it down. It created as many trading possibilities as the home mortgage market in the United States could generate. When it ran out of home loans to bundle, it started creating a seemingly limitless amount of "synthetic" trading instruments that merely referenced an already existing bundle of mortgages.

If the financial markets are like a casino, as some have suggested, then what we witnessed during the financial crisis was Wall Street's biggest stakes bettors wagering staggering sums on a three-card monte game in the back room. Some firms like Bear Stearns and Merrill Lynch and Lehman came out of the back room battered and driven into bankruptcy. Some got out of their long bets just in time. Others, including hedge fund gurus like John Paulson and Mike Bury, made billions betting short at the right time. The smart firms like Goldman Sachs won on the long side of the trades and then shifted nimbly to win on the short side too. Seldom has the world witnessed such a frenzied and sustained orgy of speculation. No other game seemed as much fun or commanded as much trading talent.

By now we all know that because of the moral-hazard-inducing principle of "too big to fail" and the $700 billion government bailout, Wall Street was betting with other people's money, namely the public's money. However, as upsetting as the raw cost of the bailout was, just as disturbing was the negative impact of Wall Street's obsession on the vitality of free markets. To be sure, there were still some large-scale deals going on such as mergers and acquisitions and initial public offerings (IPO) of profitable enterprises. Analysts were still valuing the assets of railroad companies and fiber optic manufacturers. Bankers were still evaluating the prospects of factories in New England, the Midwest, the South and the Southwest, seeking to retool and compete in the global market place. There were just not as many bankers, not as talented, and with not as much capital as was being bet in the back room.

It was not only the trading arms of financial firms that became obsessed. Even the underwriting component of Wall Street was sucked into McMansion finance. MBS underwriting grew at a staggering rate from 2000 through 2006 (Figure 2.2).

Wall Street Values

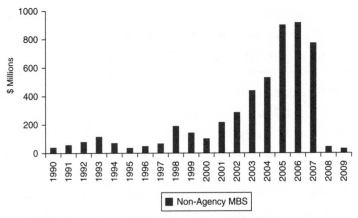

Figure 2.2. *Non-agency MBS underwriting, 1990–2009.*
Source: Securities Industry and Financial Markets Association (SIFMA).

Wall Street's firms were not content with trading MBS generated by the government-sponsored entities Freddie Mac and Fannie Mae. To feed the beast that the MBS market had become, Wall Street firms became increasingly involved with buying subprime mortgages from loan originators such as Countywide, New Century, and Ameriquest, pooling them into tranches with putatively varying levels of risk and selling them to investors, effectively cutting Freddie Mac and Fannie Mae out of the deals. (Another now well-understood part of this story was how rating agencies like Moody's and Standard &

Poor's became coconspirators in creating the housing bubble by their craven and incompetent rating of MBS deals.) So eager, in fact, were some Wall Street firms to insure deal flow in MBS that they went even deeper into the supply chain by purchasing subprime mortgage originators. In 2006, Merrill Lynch paid $1.3 billion for First Franklin.[15] Wall Street's capital was thus directly invested in mortgage lenders that inflated the housing bubble, making risky, often poorly documented, and sometimes predatory loans.

Wall Street's Role in Capital Misallocation

Wall Street was hardly a naïve and innocent bystander in this massive misallocation of capital. It was squarely to blame for the size of the bubble, the length of time it took for the markets to detect it, and the enduring impact on the economy. But for its deep self-interest in promoting collateralized debt obligations based on residential mortgages, Wall Street would most certainly have done a better job of being capitalism's "cop on the beat" and helped burst the housing bubble sooner. Wall Street, however, does not police itself as vigorously as it does others. We got a small taste of the risk of Wall Street's weak market self-enforcement during the "tech bubble" in the early 2000s. Then, Wall Street was the eager enabler of spectacular capital overinvestment in new telecommunications and Internet start-up IPOs. The damage done by the tech bubble was limited, however, by the investment banking underwriting fees that Wall Street could earn the old-fashioned way – IPO by IPO. Fast-forward to the housing bubble when Wall Street was earning most of its profits from proprietary trading and we get the super-charged version of capital misallocation. Bubbles induced by proprietary trading can, as we witnessed during the 2008 financial crisis, be larger and more lethal than those caused by IPO-induced bubbles.

To be sure, Wall Street does put some cops on its own beat. As in any other industry, the market values Wall Street firms by their performance. The shares of publicly held firms are actively traded. Financial analysts at one firm assess the financial results and prospects of rival firms. Lehman sizes up Goldman, Morgan sizes up Merrill, Goldman sizes up Morgan, and so forth. Even privately held hedge funds that do not need to publicly report their earnings are accountable to their often-sophisticated investors and the banks that finance their various trading activities. Market discipline, theoretically, could work as well on Wall Street as in any other industry to elicit socially useful outcomes from profit-maximizing behavior. However, we learned in the financial crisis that market discipline did not work effectively. There was a massive profit disjunction directly resulting in the longest economic recession in the past seven decades. The risk of such a market disjunction has steadily risen in the past three decades as a result of the transformation (described in Chapter four) of Wall Street's business model from a mostly customer orientation with a relatively small proprietary trading component to one in which trading has come to dominate the profit structure and, perhaps just as importantly, the attention of the brightest minds in the financial industry. Wall Street's inability to police itself has had a deep and enduring negative impact on the free markets and capitalism. The legacy of the financial crisis has been socially destabilizing long-term unemployment, economic malaise, and stunted growth. The obsessive-compulsive attention Wall Street lavished on the MBS market diverted capital and financial acumen from growth opportunities that would have benefited the economy as a whole and created more and better jobs. In particular, the damage fell upon two particularly vulnerable groups: new businesses and blue-collar laborers such as those in the construction industry.

Bubbles and Vacuums: How Wall Street Hurt Entrepreneurs

The flip side of an economic bubble is that resources are sucked away from more productive sectors where there is a capital "vacuum." In the years leading up to the financial crisis, Wall Street helped funnel capital and talent to the housing market, depriving companies and industries that would have deployed these otherwise available scarce resources more productively. The cost of the bailout to taxpayers was massive, but arguably more pernicious was the damage Wall Street caused to the capital markets and to the prospects of new businesses in particular. The subsequent correction created panic as it dried up all types of funding sources for nearly every kind of business and every economic sector. Half a decade later the world's capital markets have not yet recovered from the damage inflicted by Wall Street.

New firms were particularly vulnerable to the shortage of capital. It is always difficult, of course, to demonstrate "what might have been" historically. We do not know the name of the next Steve Jobs who might still be thanklessly working away in his parents' garage. The companies and executives that might have been spectacular successes are nameless casualties of Wall Street's mortgage-based securities binge. Nevertheless, there is

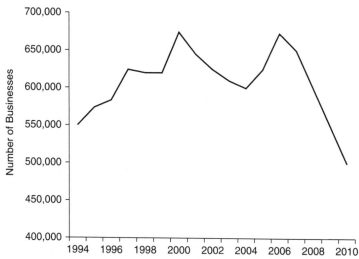

Figure 2.3. *Number of businesses less than one year old, March 1994 to March 2010.*
Source: Bureau of Labor Statistics.

some data to help us measure the magnitude of the negative impact the misallocation of capital had on new business formation. For example, the U.S. Bureau of Labor Statistics reported a significant decline in the number of business establishments less than one year old – from around 660,000 in 2006 to just over 500,000 in 2010, a decline of just under 25 percent (Figure 2.3).

Global data show a similar decline in new business formation. A 2010 World Bank working paper charts the

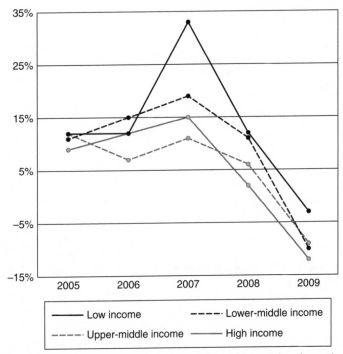

Figure 2.4. *One-year growth (percentage change) in new firm formations by national income groupings.*
Source: Klapper, L., and Love, I. (2010). The impact of the financial crisis on new firm registration. World Bank Policy Research Working Paper 5444.

decline of new business formations globally in the post-financial crisis period. All country groupings, regardless of overall national income level, experienced a sharp

Does Wall Street Have Any Responsibility to Society?

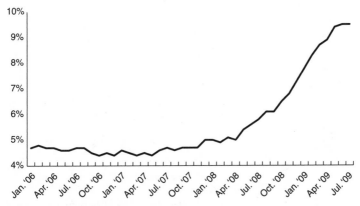

Figure 2.5. *Unemployment rate.*
Source: Bureau of Labor Statistics.

drop in new business formation in the post-crisis era (Figure 2.4).

How Wall Street Failed Workers

The damage Wall Street inflicted on labor markets was multifaceted. It is obvious but worth emphasizing that the post-crisis economic recession has led to socially corrosive levels of unemployment and underemployment (Figure 2.5).

Adding to the hardship has been an alarmingly sharp increase in the average number of weeks workers have

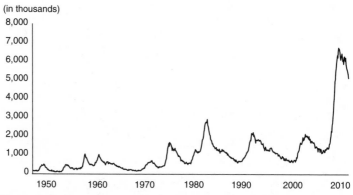

Figure 2.6. *Unemployment for 27 weeks or more, 1950–2010.*
Source: Bureau of Labor Statistics.

remained unemployed, from twelve weeks in 2001
to over thirty-five weeks in 2009. By 2010 over 7 million Americans had been unemployed for twenty-seven
weeks or more, as compared to less than 1 million in
2000 (Figure 2.6).

As devastating as the effects of the financial crisis have
been on the economy and workers, the moral connections between Wall Street and ordinary workers can be
more tightly drawn still. Blue-collar workers, in particular, are particularly vulnerable to faulty signaling in the
capital markets. Wall Street caused great harm to workers
by failing to send accurate signals to labor markets. As a

result, many individuals made life choices about where to work and what kind of work to do based on faulty information. Had Wall Street profits not been so dependent on creating and sustaining the housing bubble, Wall Street would have been better able to serve its traditional role as a dispenser of market discipline and send a signal through the market that there was a housing bubble. Instead, just when Wall Street and the capital markets should have been signaling a stop to the housing market in 2006 and 2007, Wall Street was semaphoring to move ahead.

How many workers would have made different decisions about what training to acquire, what jobs to pursue, and to what regions of the country to move if Wall Street had done a better job of signaling to the market? Hundreds of thousands? More? It is difficult to pinpoint precisely what this number might be. We can, however, acquire some appreciation for the harm Wall Street caused by examining the construction industry, where unemployment reached 25 percent by late 2009. (In some regions such as the South and the West, the rate was as high as 35 percent.) Unlike the companies that were never formed as a result of the financial crisis, these unemployed workers are not all nameless and faceless. They include people like California resident and concrete foundation worker Valentin Marquez, 41 years old and

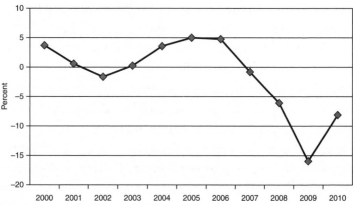

Figure 2.7. *Percentage change in employment in the construction industry, 2000–2010. Not seasonally adjusted.*
Source: Bureau of Labor Statistics.

father of four, who was out of work for a year, and his colleague Alonzo Chavez, 34 years old, who took a job in a burrito factory at minimum wage. As *Time* magazine put it, "in the southwest, the construction site is what the factory floor is to the Midwest – the place where blue collar men and women earn their keep."[16]

If you were a blue collar worker entering the job force after the turn of the century, many market signals suggested getting involved in housing construction and renovation. A decade later the decision that an individual worker made to enter the job market as a construction worker – rather than to seek further education or training in another field – was obviously riskier than he or she might have thought.[17] It is particularly troubling that many of the workers who responded to Wall Street's faulty information may have missed a generational chance to equip themselves and their families with the training they need to find employment in the post-crisis economy (Figure 2.7).

Conclusion: Socially Irresponsible Even by the Lowest Standard

The casino games played on Wall Street have vast social repercussions. Ordinary citizens and workers suffer when capital is misallocated. This is why Milton Friedman regarded the efficient functioning of free markets with such moral fervor. Capitalism can be brutal enough to winners and losers when it is functioning efficiently. But it is unnecessarily cruel when the system is inefficient. During the years leading up to the financial crisis, Wall Street was anathema to free markets. Capital was diverted away from new businesses that drove innovation and economic growth. Ordinary working people are suffering still from Wall Street's AWOL status in the capitalist system.

We began our analysis by describing a minimalist conception of corporate social responsibility. According to this view, the sole social responsibility of business is to increase profits. What we saw, however, was that the economic rules underpinning this minimalist conception do not apply to the modern financial industry. Wall Street fails the social responsibility test by its own criteria and according to the lowest standard of measurement.

How did Wall Street's business model transform itself from being primarily dedicated to client services to one where gambling with a firm's own capital became the central focus and principal source of profits? Before we answer this question by looking at developments in the financial industry, we need to examine the role of government in shaping the modern financial industry.

PART TWO

Wall Street Business Model, Regulation, and Values in Transition

— ❖ CHAPTER THREE ❖ —

The Gathering Storm: Government Missteps and Inattentiveness Contribute to the Financial Crisis

Still, if you will not fight for the right when you can easily win without bloodshed, if you will not fight when your victory will be sure and not so costly, you may come to the moment when you will have to fight with all the odds against you and only a precarious chance for survival.

Sir Winston Churchill, *The Gathering Storm* (1948)

We do not accept the view that regulators lacked the power to protect the financial system. They had ample power in many arenas and they chose not to use it. To give just three examples: the Securities and Exchange Commission could have required more capital and halted risky practices at the big investment banks. It did not. The Federal Reserve Bank of New York and other regulators could have clamped down on Citigroup's excesses in the run-up to the crisis. They did not. Policy makers and regulators could have stopped the runaway mortgage securitization train. They did not. In case after case after case, regulators continued to rate the institutions they oversaw as safe and sound even in the face of mounting troubles, often downgrading them just before their collapse. And where regulators lacked authority, they could have sought it. Too often, they lacked the political will – in a political and ideological environment that constrained it – as well as the fortitude to critically challenge the institutions and the entire system they were entrusted to oversee.

The Financial Crisis Inquiry Commission Report (2011)

Introduction: Ideology Overwhelms Experience

The financial crisis sprang from two mutually reinforcing institutional transformations – one on Wall Street and another in Washington. Fueled by an explosive mix of megamergers, massive capital formation, increased leverage, and runaway technical wizardry, the Wall Street business model evolved from providing a diversified mix of financial services for valued clients to one dominated by the investment of a firm's own capital in increasingly complex and risky securities, often at the expense of a firm's customers who came to be viewed as counterparties. The most telltale sign of Wall Street's transformation was the exponential growth and increasing importance of precisely the kind of proprietary trading, particularly of CMOs, at the center of the financial crisis. Facilitating all this was a parallel retreat in Washington's oversight of the financial industry. A succession of ideologically driven legislative and regulatory changes enabled Wall Street's increasing drive for growth in proprietary profits and introduced ever-increasing risk into the financial system. The repeal in 1999 of the Glass-Steagall Act allowed Wall Street investment banks to merge with commercial banks and insurance companies. The Commodity Futures Modernization Act of 2000 opened the floodgates for over-the-counter swap transactions including credit default swaps, and green-lighted the expansion of unregulated derivative securities. These two legislative accommodations, when combined with liberal leverage ratios and loose mortgage lending standards, enabled Wall Street to dramatically expand the scale and risk of their operations. The federal government's diminishing and ultimately irrelevant regulatory oversight of the financial markets created exponentially larger risks for the economy. There was less and less government oversight of Wall Street until all at once during the financial crisis the government would have to become involved at a previously unimaginable scale and cost to ordinary citizens.

In Chapter Four we describe the transformation of the Wall Street business model and its role in the financial crisis. In this chapter, we focus on the role of government. We consider two distinct time periods during which the government failed to safeguard the public interest. (See Figure 3.1) The first – the "Financial Deregulation Era" – extends from the mid-1980s on through to approximately mid-summer 2005. It was during this period that the federal government abandoned financial industry rules and regulatory institutions dating back over a half-century to the Great Depression. The second time frame – the "Negligent Oversight Phase" – is a roughly three-year period from the summer of 2005 until the financial crisis erupted in September 2008. During this second period, the government was grossly negligent in failing to heed and respond to loud and clear signals of the impending collapse, thereby dramatically increasing the ultimate costs to taxpayers. In fact, we argue, had the government done a better job of responding to the gathering storm in this second phase, the $700 billion taxpayer-funded bailout would have been unnecessary.

The Financial Deregulation Era (1984–2005)

Financial market deregulation stemmed from a broader trend dating back to the presidency of Ronald Reagan, continuing on through two Bush Administrations, with

The Gathering Storm

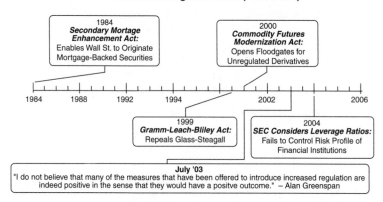

Financial Deregulation Era (1984–2005)

1984
Secondary Mortage Enhancement Act:
Enables Wall St. to Originate Mortgage-Backed Securities

2000
Commodity Futures Modernization Act:
Opens Floodgates for Unregulated Derivatives

1984   1988   1992   1994   2002   2006

1999
Gramm-Leach-Bliley Act:
Repeals Glass-Steagall

2004
SEC Considers Leverage Ratios:
Fails to Control Risk Profile of Financial Institutions

July '03
"I do not believe that many of the measures that have been offered to introduce increased regulation are indeed positive in the sense that they would have a positve outcome." – Alan Greenspan

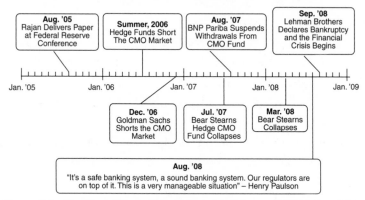

Negligent Oversight Phase (August 2005–September 2008)

Aug. '05
Rajan Delivers Paper at Federal Reserve Conference

Summer, 2006
Hedge Funds Short The CMO Market

Aug. '07
BNP Pariba Suspends Withdrawals From CMO Fund

Sep. '08
Lehman Brothers Declares Bankruptcy and the Financial Crisis Begins

Jan. '05   Jan. '06   Jan. '07   Jan. '08   Jan. '09

Dec. '06
Goldman Sachs Shorts the CMO Market

Jul. '07
Bear Stearns Hedge CMO Fund Collapses

Mar. '08
Bear Stearns Collapses

Aug. '08
"It's a safe banking system, a sound banking system. Our regulators are on top of it. This is a very manageable situation" – Henry Paulson

Figure 3.1. *Timeline of Flawed Government Policies and Failed Oversight Contributing to the Financial Crisis.*

the intervening Democratic Clinton presidency following in lockstep with Republican deregulatory ideology. Whatever the benefits of less government in other areas of commerce such as aviation, trucking, and telecommunications, in the financial sector, deregulation and the ideology of less government was a colossal disaster. When the deregulation movement began during the Reagan presidency, it was primarily based on economic principles and empirical evidence of the superior economic outcomes that could be achieved by eliminating government involvement in the private sector.[1] Eventually, however, the ideology of deregulation morphed into a radicalism that overwhelmed common sense and reliance on experience.

The fervor for financial deregulation was bipartisan. When the opportunity arose during the Clinton Administration to overhaul the regulatory regime to keep pace with a rapidly evolving financial industry, ideological hubris trumped common sense and opened the floodgates for the massively scaled and risky market in derivatives that eventually led to the financial crisis. Some regulators such as Brooksley Born, former head of the Commodities Futures Trading Commission, and academics such as Harvard Law Professor Elizabeth Warren, expressed strong concerns about shoddy mortgage-lending practices and the systemic risk building up in the financial system. However, their prescient warnings were ridiculed and shouted down by a smug and ideologically intoxicated financial plutocracy led by U.S. Treasury Secretary Robert Rubin, Federal Reserve Board Chairman Alan Greenspan, and National Economic Council head Larry Summers. Even the bipartisan Financial Crisis Inquiry Commission appointed by Congress pinned substantial blame for the crisis on the federal government's ideological fixation with deregulation. In their final report to Congress issued on January 27, 2011, the ten-member commission (with one Republican-appointed dissenter) concluded:

Widespread failures in financial regulation and supervision proved devastating to the stability of the nation's financial markets. The sentries were not at their posts, in no small part due to the widely accepted faith in the self-correcting nature of the markets and the ability of financial institutions to effectively police themselves. More than 30 years of deregulation and reliance on self-regulation by financial institutions, championed by former Federal Reserve chairman Alan Greenspan and others, supported by successive administrations and Congresses, and actively pushed by the powerful financial industry at every turn, had stripped away key safeguards, which could have helped avoid catastrophe.[2]

Three legislative developments formed the watermarks of the Financial Deregulation Era: (1) permitting the direct participation of Wall Street firms in the origination of mortgage-backed securities, resulting in the dramatic expansion of the mortgage market; (2) tearing down the long-standing wall between investment and commercial banking, which increased systemwide financial risks; and (3) removing derivative securities from federal oversight and thereby obfuscating crucial information about systemic market risk. Together these three regulatory reforms created exponentially higher system risk for the financial markets and severely hampered the abilities of the government to monitor and reduce that risk.

Financial Deregulation I: Growth and Transformation of the Mortgage Industry

While mortgages can be traced back as far as twelfth-century England and to pioneer days in seventeenth-century America, the modern-day mortgage with a standard amortization extending to thirty years came about as part of President Franklin Delano Roosevelt's post-Depression New Deal policy to encourage home ownership. The Federal Housing Administration (FHA) was created in 1934 to insure mortgage lenders against losses from nonpayment on mortgages conforming to FHA standards. In 1938, the Federal National Mortgage Association (Fannie Mae) was also established. Fannie Mae purchased FHA-insured loans from lending institutions, pooled them together, and sold them as securities on the financial markets, thereby replenishing bank liquidity while creating a secondary mortgage market for investors.

For some three decades, Fannie Mae controlled virtually the entire secondary mortgage market. In 1968, Fannie Mae split into two separate institutions: a private corporation and a publicly financed institution. The private corporation was still called Fannie Mae while a publicly financed institution – the Government National Mortgage Association (Ginnie Mae) – was formed to help finance additional housing. Ginnie Mae guaranteed the repayments of securities backed by mortgages made to government employees or veterans. The Ginnie Mae guaranty is in turn backed by the full faith and credit of the U.S. Government.[3] In an effort to provide competition for the newly private Fannie Mae and to further increase the availability of funds to finance mortgages and home ownership, Congress established a second government-sponsored enterprise (GSE), the Federal Home Loan Mortgage Corporation (Freddie Mac) as a private corporation. The activities of Freddie Mac were similar to those of Fannie Mae's, that is, buying and pooling mortgages made by savings and loan associations and other depository institutions and then selling the resulting CMOs to investors.

Wall Street Values

Traditionally, Wall Street firms acted as intermediaries, selling CMOs originated by GSEs to clients who wanted to invest in debt securities. The mortgage business was one of several product lines within the "fixed income" bond business and a minor part of overall profits. That began to change in the late 1970s when Wall Street firms became the issuers of debt securities, packaging and selling CMOs and other kinds of CDOs based on credit card debt and automobile financing. Wall Street was now in competition with Freddie Mac and Fannie Mae. Wall Street's direct involvement in issuing debt securities led to significant financial innovation and more precise configurations of risk and potential financial return. Wall Street firms could "slice and dice" the cash flows of mortgages, credit cards, and other debt instruments. These debt securities enabled investors to calibrate and customize the risk to return trade-offs they desired in their portfolios. Consumers and home buyers enjoyed increased access to mortgage and credit card debt.

Initially, the market for non-GSE-originated CMOs was small, but it exploded after the passage of the Secondary Mortgage Market Enhancement Act (SMMEA) in 1984. SMMEA allowed federal and state regulated financial institutions to invest in mortgage-backed securities. Salomon Brothers executive Lewis Ranieri reportedly was in the Oval Office when President Reagan signed the legislation.[4] After the passage of SMMEA, the CMO market expanded to include securities issued by non-GSEs so long as they were certified as investment grade by a rating agency such as Moody's or Standard & Poor's.

By the turn of the twenty-first century, securitizing of mortgages had become so lucrative that some Wall Street firms even acquired lending institutions so as to assure a steady deal flow. The growth of the securitization market represented a substantial change in the Wall Street business model. Wall Street was now in direct competition with clients Fannie Mae and Freddie Mac for CMO business. As "originators" of CMOs, Wall Street firms were engaging in principal transactions for their own accounts. Wall Street firms acted as both issuer and underwriter. They were creating debt securities and selling them to clients based upon the recommendations of their own research analysts.

To continue to grow the mortgage-backed securities business, a steady supply of newly originated mortgage loans was necessary. For the first decade or so almost all securitization activity – be it originations, structuring, or trading of these securities – was in mortgages that would be characterized as prime, that is, loans to creditworthy borrowers roughly conforming to the mortgage suitability standards set by GSEs.[5] By 2006, however, non-GSE origination of $1.480 trillion was more than 45 percent larger than GSE origination, and non-GSE issuance of $1.033 trillion was 14 percent larger than agency issuance of $905 billion.[6] No Wall Street executive wanted a highly profitable securitization machine idle, and this, in part, led beginning in around 2004, to the massive push into the next level down of credit – subprime mortgages.

Whether there was a customer on the buy side or not, the securitization creation machine would roll on – originating and bundling together mortgages, more more of them subprime. What could not be sold would be warehoused in the inventory of the Wall Street firms. For several years, largely as a result of macroeconomic factors – including the movement of interest rates, the frothy housing market, and the pricing of credit – this warehousing activity yielded profits for Wall Street firms. Fannie Mae and Freddie Mac, too, eagerly built up inventory of their own CMOs. Eventually, however the housing and CMO markets came crashing down, resulting in the bankruptcy of Lehman Brothers, financial exigency for other financial institutions, and the government takeover of Fannie Mae and Freddie Mac.

In addition to enacting SMMEA in 1984, other government policies also contributed to the housing bubble and eventual collapse of the mortgage market. Former Federal Reserve Board member Dr. Susan Phillips expressed the view that "government encouraged household mortgage expansion ... held interest rates low in the early part of the decade after the dot com crash and ... may have encouraged many to take on mortgages they could not handle. Regulators were also slow to recognize the dangers of lowering the household mortgage underwriting standards."[7] The Financial Crisis Inquiry Commission echoed Dr. Phillips's conclusion, citing in particular, "the Federal Reserve's pivotal failure to stem the flow of toxic mortgages, which it could have done by setting prudent mortgage-lending standards. The Federal Reserve was the one entity empowered to do so and it did not."[8]

Financial Deregulation II: Tearing Down the Wall Between Commercial and Investment Banking

In 1999 President Bill Clinton signed the Gramm-Leach-Bliley Act into law, thereby repealing the 1933 Glass-Steagall Act's prohibition preventing commercial banks from engaging in the investment banking or insurance businesses. The repeal of Glass-Steagall gave Wall Street access to new sources of capital and, conversely, allowed commercial banks and insurance companies to operate on Wall Street. Traditional Wall

Street firms could get bigger, and big commercial banks and insurance companies could now become Wall Street players. Citicorp epitomized the new breed of financial services "supermarket" combining Citibank's commercial bank with the Travelers Insurance Company and the Salomon Smith Barney securities trading and investment banking franchise. So confident were the parties of the deregulatory zeitgeist that they consummated the merger in 1998, fully a year before the repeal was enacted into law.

The mergers and acquisitions made possible by the repeal of Glass-Steagall also created risk for assets that since 1933 had been cordoned off from the risks associated with the vicissitudes of Wall Street and the capital markets. As the U.S. Supreme Court noted in a 1971 case:

The legislative history of the Glass-Steagall Act shows that Congress also had in mind and repeatedly focused on the more subtle hazards that arise when a commercial bank goes beyond the business of acting as fiduciary or managing agent and enters the investment banking business either directly or by establishing an affiliate to hold and sell particular investments. This course places new promotional and other pressures on the bank which, in turn, create new temptations.[9]

As if it were not reckless enough to herd commercial banking and insurance companies into the Wall Street firmament, the SEC contributed to systemic risk by failing to rein in the largest investment banks as they increased their total borrowings relative to capital.[10] This relationship, which is known as a firm's leverage ratio, was as high as 40 to 1 at some firms in the years proceeding the financial crisis, meaning that $40 was borrowed for every $1 of capital. In 2004, the SEC promulgated several reforms regarding leverage ratios, but failed to address the increasing systemic risk.[11]

Regulators and legislators from both the Democratic and Republican parties promoted reforms enabling Wall Street firms to expand their capital base, increase their use of leverage, and broaden the varieties of trading and other principal transactions they could engage in to generate revenue. These reforms catalyzed a dramatic expansion of scale. For a time, the resulting profits were prodigious and used, in part, to grease the politicians' reelection campaigns. And thus, when Wall Street eventually became fixated on trading derivative securities, Washington again would prove to be an accommodating friend.

Financial Deregulation III: Forestalling Government Oversight of Derivative Securities

Thanks to the Commodity Futures Modernization Act (CFMA) signed into law by President Clinton in 2000,

Wall Street had no trouble finding investment vehicles for its newfound leverage capacity.[12] The CFMA, devised by a joint presidential commission including Wall Street professionals and Washington regulators (many of whom had worked in the financial industry), removed over-the-counter (i.e., non-exchange traded) futures transactions between sophisticated parties from oversight by the Commodities Futures Trading Commission (CFTC). The net result was a green light for significant expansion of derivatives, including the credit default swaps (CDS) at the heart of the financial crisis. A CDS allowed one firm exposed to the credit risk of a particular mortgage-backed security, or for that matter to almost any credit risk, to purchase insurance to protect against loss from the credit exposure. The proliferation of CDSs increased systemic risk and interconnectivity.[13] Perhaps the most troubling aspect of the CFMA was that Washington blithely enacted the legislation just two years after the $3.625 billion bailout of Long-Term Capital Management organized by the Federal Reserve Board of New York among Wall Street firms. CFTC Commissioner Brooksley Born voiced opposition to the proposed deregulation. Born correctly understood that the CFMA would hide the derivatives market from public oversight precisely at the moment when the systemic risks for the financial markets were mounting. "The

CFTC is currently the only federal agency with statutory authority over hedge funds like Long-Term Capital Management and over a significant portion of the swaps market," Born testified, and "to tie its hands during this time of economic instability and growing awareness of the potential dangers in the swaps market could pose grave risks to the American public."[14] Born was shouted down however, by a cackle of Clinton administration officials including Treasury Secretary Robert Rubin, Federal Reserve Board Chair Alan Greenspan, National Economic Council head Larry Summers, and SEC Chair Arthur Levitt, just as private derivatives contracts began a new round of explosive growth (Figure 3.2).

Testifying to a Senate subcommittee in 2003, Alan Greenspan was characteristically expansive and turgid in describing the putative virtues of deregulating a financial market that within a few years would bring the global financial system to its knees and require a $700 billion government bailout:

What we have found over the years in the marketplace is that derivatives have been an extraordinarily useful vehicle to transfer risk from those who should not be taking it to those who are willing to take it and are capable of doing so.... My concern and others' concerns about going in the direction of an increasing degree of Government regulation is that we will undercut counterparty surveillance and that the net effect will not be to enhance the stability of that overall structure, but undermine it, and it has become such a valuable tool,

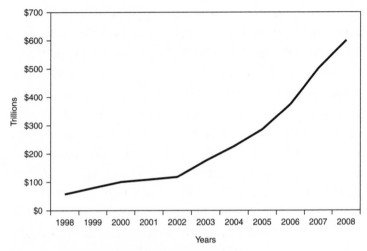

Figure 3.2. *Private derivative contracts explode.*
Source: Bank for International Settlements.

in my judgment, in the international financial system that anything that we can do to enhance its capability of internal stabilization, which is currently the case, we ought to do, and I do not believe that many of the measures that have been offered to introduce increased regulation are indeed positive in the sense that they would have a positive outcome.[15]

Why Greenspan thought that government regulation would reduce private due diligence is not clear. In fact, contrary to Greenspan's unsubstantiated assertion, the lack of regulation did not propel the banks and rating agencies to great heights of "surveillance."

By 2008, the notional amount of CDSs held by financial institutions approximated $60 trillion on a gross level, and has been estimated by some at $14 trillion on a net settlement basis. To put this number in perspective, the production of the entire U.S. economy is $14 trillion per year, and the federal budget is $3.6 trillion. Citigroup was emblematic of the risk expansion resulting from repeal of the Glass-Steagall Act, liberalization of capital-debt ratios, and deregulation of CDSs. One small trading unit within the company was able to amass a "long" trading position in mortgage-backed securities that was so large and lost so much money that it wiped out virtually the entire capital base of Citibank commercial bank, Travelers Insurance, and the Salomon Smith Barney investment bank combined. When the financial crisis struck in the fall of 2008, Citicorp was saved from bankruptcy by becoming the single largest recipient of funds from the $700 billion taxpayer-funded bailout. AIG was a prime buyer of credit risk or seller of credit insurance through the CDS format and, in the process, became a repository of enormous risk. It was only in the heat of the financial crisis that the U.S. government determined that it would be catastrophic for the overall financial system if AIG failed, and thus seized control of AIG on September 16, 2008.[16] It should be noted that ultimately the prime beneficiaries of the

AIG rescue were the banks, for example, Citicorp and Goldman Sachs, that owned the other side of the CDS contracts held by AIG.

The Negligent Oversight Phase (2005–2008)

As we have seen, during the Financial Deregulation Era, lasting from roughly 1984 to 2004, the U.S. government helped bring about the financial crisis by dismantling half-century-old regulatory institutions and rules to accommodate Wall Street business interests. The end result was to generate exponentially larger systemwide risk and to create such interconnectivitiy that the failure of a few significant financial institutions would threaten the viability of virtually every major Wall Street firm. Government was the chief enabler of a financial industry that had become too big and too interconnected to fail. Besides helping to create the conditions for the financial crisis, a less well-understood failure of government was its inexplicable failure during the Negligent Oversight Phase – lasting from roughly the summer of 2005 to September 2008 – to hear the loud alarms sounding about the dangers lurking in the mortgage market and the overall risk level of financial markets.

The financial crisis crept upon ordinary citizens seemingly overnight and with little warning. However, many

Wall Street insiders and government economists had been forewarned that an economic reckoning was coming as early as the summer of 2005 – more than three years prior to September 2008 when U.S. Treasury Secretary Henry Paulson came to the belated realization that the world financial system was "on the brink" (to borrow a phrase from the title of Paulson's memoirs) of collapse. Despite claims by Greenspan, Paulson, and other government officials that they understood and reacted to the gathering storm competently and in a timely manner, the Financial Crisis Inquiry Commission concluded that "key policy makers – the Treasury Department, the Federal Reserve Board, and the Federal Reserve Bank of New York – who were best positioned to watch over our markets were ill prepared for the events of 2007 and 2008."[17] But, when did the global economy arrive "on the brink"? When might we say definitively that the government "should have known" that we were in a crisis and acted more decisively? Three pivotal moments, prior to September 2008, spring to mind as possibilities for when government officials might have appreciated the imminence and magnitude of the coming crisis.

Pivotal Moment #1. August 2005 – When the Smartest People Knew. In August 2005 Raghuran G. Rajan, the chief economist at the International Monetary Fund, delivered a paper in Jackson Hole, Wyoming, to a conference sponsored by the Federal Reserve Bank of Kansas City. Larry Summers, Robert Rubin, and Alan Greenspan were in attendance, as were many other leading economists in government and industry. Rajan questioned the prevailing orthodoxy that the federal government's hands-off policy toward the financial industry was reducing systemic risk by allowing it to be dispersed among market participants. What Rajan found from looking at the data was that banks were getting riskier at the same time that they were distributing risk to their clients. Logically, this could mean only one thing to Rajan – that the system as a whole must be getting more, not less, risky. Larry Summers, then in the final stages of his controversial and brief stint as president of Harvard, rose to proclaim "the basic, slightly Luddite premise of this paper to be largely misguided."[18] Such was the enormous faith the economic plutocrats had in their ideology of financial deregulation that they responded to Rajan's logic and evidence-based claims with name-calling and intellectual bullying, just as they had once done with CFTC Commissioner Brooksley Born when she had warned about the dangers of deregulating the derivatives market.

It is perhaps too high a standard to suggest that government regulators should have anticipated and done something about the impending crisis in August 2005 when Raghuran Rajan sounded the initial alarms. Nonetheless, others in government and academia did recognize the systemic risks building in the system. In 2002, Sheila Bair, then assistant secretary for Financial Institutions at the Treasury Department, attempted to argue for greater vigilance over mortgage loan documentation but was quietly brushed out of office for her apostasy. Harvard Law professor Elizabeth Warren warned that overly aggressive lending practices were drawing financially stressed consumers into burdensome mortgage obligations. State regulators, closer to economic realities, in some respects did a better job of comprehending the gathering storm than did their Washington counterparts. In 2005, forty-nine states and the District of Columbia won a $325 million class action suit against lending institutions for deceptive mortgage origination practices.[19] Among those paying attention to Rajan's empirical claims were a number of hedge fund managers who early in 2006 sharpened their pencils and technical analysis and began to see the impending collapse of the mortgage market – people like Steve Eisman and Mike Burry described by Michael Lewis in *The Big Short* and John Paulson whom Gregory Zuckerman profiled in *The Greatest Trade Ever*.[20] These investors saw through the triple-A ratings and the hype around mortgage-backed securities and shorted the market in 2006, earning them enormous gains when the market soured in 2007.

Pivotal Moment #2. December 2006 – When Henry Paulson's Former Colleagues at Goldman Sachs Knew. In December 2006 Paulson's former employer Goldman Sachs realized that it was dangerously overinvested in mortgage debt securities. As described in Chapter Five, by May 2007 the firm had successfully unwound its long position and adopted an aggressively short position that would earn $17 billion in profits in 2007, a year when the rest of Wall Street was experiencing record losses. Might the government be reasonably expected to understand the impending threats when Goldman Sachs understood the dangers? Again, this is perhaps too high a standard to expect. Still, however, it is worth ruminating a bit on the Goldman Sachs connection and what might have been.

Since Robert Rubin was appointed Treasury Secretary in the Clinton Administration, Goldman Sachs alumni have bestrode the corridors of power in Washington. Henry Paulson, like Rubin, served as head of the firm before being tapped to become Treasury Secretary in July 2006. Six months almost to the day after Paulson left Goldman Sachs, his old firm made a momentous decision to reverse course on the mortgage market.

Apparently, no one at Goldman Sachs thought to call their former colleague in government to inform him that the financial markets were headed for Armageddon. And Paulson apparently, with all the research resources and information available in the Treasury Department, did not sense the gathering storm as clearly as his former colleagues. A simple explanation might be that it was Goldman Sachs traders who in late 2006 came to the conclusion that the "Big Short" hedge fund managers contacting them to bet against the mortgage market might indeed possess a correct view. Henry Paulson rose to be head of Goldman Sachs from an investment banking background rather than the rough, tumble, and immediacy of the trading operations. Still, one has to wonder what the point is of having Goldman Sachs-trained people in government if they cannot deliver the same performance in public service as they do when working on Wall Street.

Pivotal Moment 3. Summer 2007 – When Just About Everyone on Wall Street Knew. Might it at least be reasonable to expect that government would have a sense of urgency about the mortgage markets when most of Wall Street knew? By the summer of 2007, leaders at every major Wall Street firm realized that the mortgage market was in dire straits and their very survival at risk. In July 2007, Bear Sterns pledged $3.2 billion in loan funds to bail out two of its funds that had invested in CDOs. On August 9, 2007, BNP Paribas stopped customer withdrawals in one of its funds because it could not determine CMO values. This was still over a year before Lehman Brothers went bankrupt and Henry Paulson acknowledged that the financial system was "on the brink" of collapse. By March 2008 the losses at Bear Sterns were so catastrophic that this Wall Street stalwart, which had survived the 1929 stock market crash without laying off any workers, could only be salvaged by an emergency loan from the New York Federal Reserve Board and a quick distress sale to JP Morgan Chase.

Although it might have been news to most ordinary citizens, all around Wall Street the carnage flowing from the collapse of the CMO market was well understood. Yet as late as the summer of 2008, Paulson and Federal Reserve Board Chairman Benjamin Bernanke were making reassuring public statements about the overall health and stability of credit markets. "It's a safe banking system, a sound banking system," Paulson told CBS news on July 20, 2008, "our regulators are on top of it. This is a very manageable situation." On August 10, 2008, Paulson told NBC's Meet the Press that he had no plans to inject capital into Freddie Mac or Fannie Mae, less than a month before he ordered them put them into government conservatorship.

Conclusion: The Financial Crisis that Never Should Have Been

When historians look back on the financial crisis decades from now, the most astonishing "what if" question will be to ask how much economic calamity and public suffering could have been averted if Paulson and others in government had understood the fragility of the financial markets at the same time (December 2006) as the firm Paulson had led only six months prior? What if the government had acted to mitigate the damage to ordinary citizens even half as nimbly as Goldman Sachs had looked out for the interests of its shareholders? Even if the government had grasped the enormity of the situation when the rest of Wall Street did in the summer of 2007, we almost certainly would have averted the massive government bailout that became necessary when the problems were allowed to fester for another year. Had the government acted at any of these three moments, there might have been no financial "crisis." A soft landing of the CMO market might have been possible instead of the thundering crash that did occur. Might the crippling economic recession that followed the financial crisis have been averted?

The government's slowness to detect and respond to the crisis is as galling as its regulatory miscalculations in helping bring it about. Instead of a measured and thought-ful government response to the rapidly deteriorating con-dition of the CMO market, what we got was panic and a paucity of remedial options. The crisis that never should have been was so sudden, so dramatic, and so frightening that there was hardly a moment to blink before Treasury Secretary Paulson cajoled Congress into authorizing a taxpayer funded government bailout of unprecedented size and scope – the $700 billion Troubled Asset Relief Program TARP. Eventually, American taxpayers had to fund a bailout of the financial industry totaling over a trillion dollars. Congress intended the treasury secre-tary to use the TARP authorization to purchase CDOs in an attempt to stabilize market prices in those securities. However, almost immediately Secretary Paulson used the money in a manner not specifically authorized by Congress. Paulson had worked as an investment banker for his entire career prior to joining the government. While at Goldman Sachs he helped companies raise capi-tal to fund operations and expansion. It should thus come as no surprise that he viewed the financial crisis as pri-marily a capital crisis for the major Wall Street firms. He and his staff quickly abandoned the tactic that Congress had authorized in funding TARP, that is, making a mar-ket for CDOs that would stem their loss of value. Instead Paulson did the one thing he had learned to do well at

Goldman Sachs – help companies raise capital. Instead of stabilizing the CDO market, he saved the firms most heavily invested in CDOs by injecting them with capital. Paulson explained his reasoning in his memoir On the Brink: "To oversimplify: assuming banks had a ten-to-one leverage ratio, injecting $70 billion in equity would give us as much impact as buying $700 billion in assets. This was the fastest way to get the most money into the banks, renew confidence in their strength, and get them lending again." Beneath portraits of George Washington and Abraham Lincoln in the Treasury Department conference room, Paulson gathered the CEOs of the largest American banks and made them an offer they could not refuse – easy money and lots of it. Citibank CEO Vikram Pandit quickly grasped the largesse that Paulson was offering to Wall Street: "I've just run the numbers. This is very cheap capital. I'm in."[21]

From Financial Services to Proprietary Trading: The Transformation of Wall Street's Business Model

Introduction

Beginning roughly in the last two decades of the twentieth century and culminating with the 2008 financial crisis, the dominant Wall Street business model transformed from a customer-driven focus with a minor proprietary trading component to one where principal transactions, and in particular trading in mortgage-backed securities, came to dominate the profits and attention of the brightest minds in the financial industry. This transformation represents a major shift in Wall Street's business model. The bulk of Wall Street's profits today are no longer derived from providing financial services to clients. Instead, Wall

Street firms generate profits mostly from investing their own capital. The rise of principal transactions occurred not coincidentally just as the financial industry was also experiencing enormous growth in scale as, in the two decades preceding the financial crisis, every major Wall Street firm went from being a privately funded partnership to a publicly held company.

In Chapter two we introduced the idea that profit disjunction occurs when the profits of Wall Street are not aligned with the prosperity of the economy as a whole. In this chapter, we examine how Wall Street profits became unhinged from and dangerous to the general welfare of society. We describe not only how Wall Street became dependent on proprietary trading and the perverse compensation incentives encouraging moral hazard and excessive risk taking, but also how Wall Street became so large that its potential failure as a business sector threatened the stability of the global economy. Our purpose in doing so is not simply to address the issue of "too big to fail" and the bailout. Our objective is to demonstrate how the shift in Wall Street's business model from serving clients to proprietary trading accompanied a crisis in Wall Street values that in no small measure contributed to the financial crisis. We are concerned, in other words, not only with the threats Wall Street poses to the general economy when it fails, but also with the dangers it creates when it is successful following the postmillennial proprietary trading business model. We begin our analysis, however, by recalling a long bygone era when ongoing customer relations, based upon trust and mutuality, were an essential foundation for the creation and success of the financial industry.

After the 1929 Stock Market Crash: Wall Street Restores Trust With Clients

The New York Stock Exchange (NYSE), now owned by Euronext, traces its roots to 1792 when twenty-four merchants and brokers signed the Buttonwood Agreement. This agreement established a formal framework for how securities brokers would conduct business with each other and their clients.[1] In effect, the American securities industry was born. Over the next 137 years the securities markets and the securities business grew and helped sustain extraordinary economic expansion and prosperity. The financial markets endured various panics, corruption, scandals, and bubbles, but they and the country bounced back relatively quickly to prosperity. The crash of 1929, however, brought the entire securities market to the cusp of extinction and drove the nation's economy into the Great Depression.

The crash and the ensuing prolonged depression, which persisted through the 1930s, severely eroded

public trust in the financial markets. Confidence was eroded not only because stock prices crashed, but also because of questionable ethical behavior by leading financial institutions and executives. Goldman Sachs Trading Corp., a closed-end mutual fund with Ponzi-like elements, was launched during the 1920s and generated substantial profits before failing in the crash and tarnishing Goldman Sach's reputation for decades.[2] Charles E. Mitchell, head of National City Bank – predecessor to today's Citibank and one of the country's largest banks – was arrested and indicted on charges of fraud.[3]

The crash and the Great Depression prompted government and private institutions to take steps to restore trust in the markets. Public legal reform of the securities industry followed a two-pronged approach: (1) attempting to assure transparency and informational symmetry in the securities markets and (2) detecting and prosecuting fraudulent behavior through private lawsuits and criminal prosecutions. Companies selling stock to the public (issuers) were required to disclose all material facts, including relevant risks. Financial firms that helped underwrite and distribute these securities were made jointly (together with issuers) and severally (i.e., they could be sued individually for the full amount of the damages) liable to investors for the issuer's misstatements. The SEC was founded in 1933 to implement and

enforce these new laws. In concert with self-regulatory bodies like the NYSE, rules were established to help assure that financial professionals would deal honestly with investors in the general public.[4] The era of customer and client focus in the securities business had begun. Post-crash legal reforms also sought to shore up confidence in commercial banks. Paramount among these efforts was the erstwhile Glass-Steagall Act mandating the separation of commercial banks from investment banks. Segregating businesses such as purchasing and holding securities and underwriting new stock offerings into the realm of investment banks was designed to disengage the vicissitudes of market risk from commercial banks, whose main functions were to promote and protect savings and to make loans.

Complementing public efforts were imaginative initiatives by private firms building successful financial services businesses around the novel concept of treating investors fairly. Charles E. Merrill, namesake of the firm Merrill Lynch and Co., helped create what proved for decades to be an innovative sustainable business model emphasizing long-term relations with customers. In his classic 1955 book *Wall Street: Men and Money*, Martin Mayer, a financial journalist and historian, describes Merrill as the catalyst for bringing the public into the financial markets "not as lambs to be slaughtered but as partners

in the benefits."[5] Merrill is credited with democratizing the stock market and contributing to the confidence middle class America came to have in the financial markets. The firm sparked a venerable host of imitators and competitors, such as Shearson, Paine Webber, and E. F. Hutton, that also made client service and honest dealing the centerpieces of their business strategies.[6]

Merrill Lynch's economic success was inextricably linked to earning client confidence and providing high-quality service. From a peak of nearly 70 percent of revenue in 1962 to just over 50 percent of revenue in 1971, aggregate commission revenues (fees paid by customers to brokerage firms for executing securities transactions) constituted the mainstay of the business. The customer focus of this era was described in the 1970 Annual Report of Merrill Lynch in quaint language that might evoke wry amusement on contemporary Wall Street:

We do not speculate with the firm's money. That means we do not invest it in common stocks except where we are market-makers; then we hold stocks in our inventory, but only for brief periods of time.... We are of course in business to make money. But if adherence to this careful philosophy of Merrill's had benefited only Merrill Lynch, those of us who direct the firm would have a sense of incompleteness. In a time when our interests and some broader interests of the public coincided more clearly than ever before, we were gratified by the knowledge that our policies served other people besides ourselves, and served them well.[7]

In the 1960s and 1970s Merrill Lynch, like other Wall Street firms, was organized as a partnership. In this partnership era the size and scale of Wall Street operations were nowhere near that of contemporary financial behemoths. Merrill, the leading firm catering to retail clients, had commission revenues of $361 million in 1971; a modest figure, even adjusted for inflation, when compared to the $31 billion in principal trading revenues accumulated by Goldman Sachs in 2007. It is important to emphasize that the traditional fixed brokerage commission revenues of Wall Street firms were deregulated in May, 1975 and one result was that these revenues came under significant price pressure from "discount" brokers such as Charles Schwab that offered "no frills" trades without personalized investment advice. The modern, proprietary trading-obsessed Wall Street firm is thus at least in part a by-product of necessity driven by the obsolescence of the old client-based business model in the closing decades of the twentieth century.

The post-crash legal and commercial reforms were effective in restoring public trust in the financial system. America and Wall Street enjoyed decades of shared prosperity. Growth and prosperity, however, beget opportunities and change. The business imperative to grow scale, scope, and profits stimulated many profound changes that would lead to a radical transformation of the financial industry. Among the most significant factors driving this change was Wall Street's newfound ability to raise capital in public markets. By the 1970s, Wall Street firms came up with a bright idea: for decades, we have been successful at raising investment capital for other industries seeking growth, they reasoned; why not tap the public markets for our own capital requirements?

Other People's Money: Wall Street Grows Bigger and Riskier

From the 1792 Buttonwood Agreement until 1970, NYSE rules prohibited firms from being owned by shareholders not actively involved in the management of the firm. Consequently, virtually every member of the NYSE was organized as a partnership. The constraints placed by the partnership structure on access to capital prevented any one institution from being "too big to fail" and offered some measure of assurance that these firms would take prudent risks to ensure the ongoing viability of the firm. In a partnership the owners/operators – that is, the partners – are personally liable for losses incurred in operations. If this responsibility alone were not enough to focus the mind on sound risk management, as noted, the post- crash securities laws created joint and several liability for financial firms acting as underwriters of public securities. This meant that if a company raising capital from the public misstated a fact or figure in the sales prospectus, the individual partners of the investment bank that helped solicit the sale of the securities on behalf of the company could be sued personally by investors for any losses related to the misstatement, unless the underwriter could show that it had performed a "due diligence" investigation of the company's operations to attempt to uncover the misstatement.

For more than forty years, the NYSE partnership rules, when combined with the potential of joint and several legal liability, established Wall Street as a crucial component of a highly effective fraud detection and risk management system for the financial markets. Wall Street became the engine room of capitalism and free markets, helping investors channel capital to investment-worthy companies that in turn created innovative products, economic growth, and jobs. It was a symbiotic relationship. When Wall Street firms did their jobs well and prospered so, too, did the economy and society. This overlap of interests between Wall Street and Main Street began to unravel in 1970, however, when the NYSE enacted a rule change allowing member firms to avail themselves of the corporate structure and raise capital through stock offerings to public shareholders.[8]

From Financial Services to Proprietary Trading

In the next thirty years virtually every major U.S. investment bank adopted the corporate legal form and raised capital from investors. The evolution of "going public" began with Donaldson, Lufkin, and Jenrette in 1970 and continued through May 1999 when Goldman Sachs became the last major Wall Street firm to make the transition. To be fair, the putative benefits of going public extended beyond investors and the Wall Street firms themselves. Augmenting the permanent capital accounts of investment banks provided increased financial strength and confidence to the firm's customers and the overall market place. As we were soon to discover all too well, however, accompanying these benefits from capital scale was a substantially increased risk to the capital markets in the form of the "moral hazard" arising when Wall Street executives were no longer putting their own personal capital at risk.

The infusion of public investment capital swelled the sheer scale of operations on Wall Street. There are many ways to illustrate this overall growth of the securities industry in last two decades of the twentieth century. Total employment at the five largest securities firms grew fourfold from 1979 to 2000. Capital investment per employee grew from a range of $27,000 to $113,000 in 1979 to a range of $875,000 to $3,585,000 in 2000.[9] The scale of the financial industry further increased with the repeal of the Glass-Steagall Act, giving Wall Street access to new sources of capital resources and conversely allowing commercial banks and insurance companies to operate on Wall Street. Citicorp epitomized the new breed of financial services "supermarket," combining commercial banking, insurance, and investment banking. By 2006 the financial sector accounted for 30 percent of U.S. corporate profits, up from 10 percent in 1986.[10] As a percentage of gross domestic product (GDP) the finance industry grew to 8.2 percent in 2006[11] (Figure 4.1).

Wall Street firms not only got much bigger. They also fundamentally changed how they did business and made profits. Traditionally, the overwhelming majority of revenues were generated principally by commissions for executing brokerage transactions, investment banking fees from the underwriting of new issues of securities for companies coming to Wall Street to raise money for their own operations, and advisory fees for mergers and acquisitions. However, the new business model sought to expand revenues by risking the firm's own capital. Wall Street firms traditionally had earned a small percentage (approximately 10 percent) from proprietary trading activities and other principal transactions such as private equity investments, but under the emerging business model these kinds of activities came to predominate.

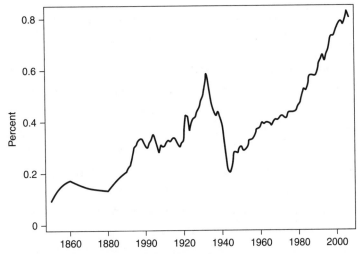

Figure 4.1. *GDP share of U.S. finance industry.*
Source: Philippon, T., and Reshef, A. (2009). NBER Working Paper No. 14644.

In the years leading up to the financial crisis, decades after this trend began, this focus on principal transactions would prove to be catastrophic. Mismanaged Wall Street firms were to become almost singularly obsessed with betting the house on mortgage-backed securities. However, when the trend began, the risk-reward opportunities created excitement for investors and Wall Street professionals alike.

Wall Street in Transition: 1980s Salomon Brothers to Postmillennial Goldman Sachs

In the roaring 1980s, Wall Street was still providing traditional brokerage and investment banking services to customers. However, those business units were becoming less important. Epitomizing this rapidly evolving business model was the firm of Salomon Brothers, whose revenues and profits from proprietary trading propelled it from a boutique firm specializing in making a market in debt securities to one of the most profitable and dynamic firms on Wall Street (Table 4.1). Even the famed "value investor" Warren Buffett was impressed enough to become the largest single investor in Salomon. By the late 1980s Salomon was paradigmatic of the new business model. It was also a precursor and prototype of the gargantuan proprietary trading operations of firms like Goldman Sachs that would come to dominate Wall Street in the twenty-first century.

The risks posed to the financial system by Wall Street's new business model should have been more alarming in 1991 when Salomon Brothers almost disappeared virtually overnight. The factors leading to Salomon's near demise uncannily foreshadowed the dynamics of the 2008 financial crisis. The firm embodied overzealous proprietary trading in debt securities driven by a

Table 4.1. *Salomon Brothers revenue 1986–1990 (in $millions)*

Year ended December 31	1986	1987	1988	1989	1990
Principal transactions	1,064	1,154	1,711	2,513	2,389
Investment banking	577	403	564	470	416
Commissions	208	266	206	226	207
Other revenues	456	207	(146)	(303)	(25)
Total revenues	2,305	2,030	2,335	2,906	2,987
Percent of Total revenues from Principal transactions	46%	57%	73%	86%	80%

Source: Salomon Brothers Annual Reports.

compensation system that encouraged excessive risk taking and the disregard of responsibilities to clients. The scandal was put in motion when Salomon trader Paul Moser placed a fraudulent bid in the United States Treasury Securities debt auction. Moser was limited to how much he could bid in the auction by Treasury Department rules. His solution was to place false bids in the names of longtime clients of the firm who were unaware that Salomon was using their names for its proprietary trading. When Moser's actions came to light, it ended the career of Salomon CEO John Gutfreund. Gutfreund later declared that he knew his career was over when he went to his front door to get the morning paper and saw his picture on the front page of the *New York Times*. The scandal caused a liquidity crunch at Salomon as other Wall Street firms sought to distance themselves. Warren Buffett eventually came to the rescue by injecting additional capital into the firm and smoothing over relations with government leaders who were outraged by Salomon's attempt to defraud and thwart the system by which the U.S. government financed its national debt. After a series of mergers Salomon eventually became part of Citigroup.[12]

The Salomon scandal was but one early warning signal of how a transforming Wall Street business model eventually would depend on exploiting, rather than caring for, customers. Both Bankers Trust and Merrill Lynch were involved in well-publicized cases that presaged the shift in values away from customer loyalty. Bankers Trust was accused of fraud by its client Procter & Gamble, which alleged deceptive sales practices and lack of full disclosure about the riskiness of an investment. Particularly damning were revelations from the internal Bankers Trust tape recording system. Discussing the profits to be made on the transaction, a Bankers Trust employee said Procter & Gamble "would never be able to know how much money was taken out ... that's the beauty of Bankers Trust."[13] The case was settled

for $200 million in May 1995. Its reputation severely tarnished, a few years later Bankers Trust was broken up and sold, with Deutsche Bank acquiring the lion's share. Even Merrill Lynch, the firm that epitomized Wall Street's client-focused business model, agreed in 1998 to settle a case involving claims of reckless investment advice and sales of toxic derivatives to Orange County.[14]

Wall Street firms such as Merrill Lynch in the 1960s and 1970s and Salomon Brothers in the 1980s were icons of their respective eras. Another iconic firm, Goldman Sachs, epitomizes the final stage in the transformation of Wall Street's business model from a mostly customer orientation with a minor proprietary trading component to one in which trading operations and other principal transactions came to dwarf customer-related revenues.

In the three years immediately preceding the financial crisis, over 75 percent of Goldman Sachs's profits were earned from trading and principal investments (Table 4.2). This compares to less than 30 percent of Goldman Sachs's revenues coming from trading and principal investments a decade earlier (Table 4.3). As we shall see in Chapter five, it was not just the economics that changed on Wall Street. Inevitably as the source of profits shifted, so too did the core values of Wall Street – from rigorous adherence to customer needs, trust, and

Table 4.2. *Goldman Sachs operating results by business segment 2005–2007 (in $millions)*

Business segment		2005	2006	2007
Investment banking	Revenues	3,671	5,629	7,555
	Pretax earnings	413	1,567	2,570
Trading and principal investments	Revenues	16,818	25,562	31,226
	Pretax earnings	6,218	10,600	13,228
Asset management and security services	Revenues	4,749	6,474	7,206
	Pretax earnings	1,679	2,438	1,843
Total	Revenues	25,238	37,665	45,987
	Pretax earnings	8,273	14,560	17,604
Percent Pretax earnings from Trading and principal investments		75%	72%	75%

Source: Goldman Sachs 2007 Annual Report.

mutuality to one of "beggar thy neighbor" where profits came from, and sometimes at the expense of clients.

Wall Street's Obsession with Mortgage-Backed Securities

The last element needed to understand the dangers posed by Wall Street's business model in the years leading up to the financial crisis was its fatal attraction to CMOs, debt

From Financial Services to Proprietary Trading

Table 4.3. *Goldman Sachs revenues by business segment 1996–1998 (in $millions)*

	1996	1997	1998
Investment banking	2,113	2,587	3,368
Trading and principal investments	2,693	2,926	2,379
Asset management and securities services	1,323	1,934	2,773
Total revenues	6,129	7,447	8,520
Percent of Total revenues from Trading and principal investments	43%	39%	28%

Source: Goldman Sachs 1998 Annual Report.

instruments backed by payments homeowners make on mortgages. Initially, Wall Street firms focused on bundling together pools of mortgages originated by other financial institutions including Fannie Mae and Freddie Mac, and selling the risks and income flows associated with the mortgages' CMOs to investors. Firms sometimes retained a small percentage of the CMOs for their own private, proprietary accounts, as had been customary for underwriters of other kinds of securities in the investment banking business. As the decade of the 2000s progressed, however, proprietary trading in CMOs and related derivative instruments came to dominate the balance sheets and profit and loss statements of Wall Street firms. This focus narrowed the scope of Wall Street's business portfolio precisely at the moment that the scale of their operations was growing exponentially. Basic portfolio theory teaches the importance of a diversified portfolio to weather investment risk. Wall Street, however, was imprudently putting all its eggs into one big basket.

Ironically, some Wall Street veterans viewed the financial sector's role in creating and marketing mortgage-backed securities as explicitly promoting a social good in the form of increased housing ownership. Indeed, when these kinds of securities were first invented at firms such as Salomon Brothers and First Boston in the 1980s, many believed that in addition to making extraordinary profits Wall Street was helping promote liquidity in the mortgage market, thereby enabling millions to achieve the American dream of homeownership. Even as late as April 2007 when the downturn in the housing market was well underway, Lewis Ranieri was trumpeting the virtues of financial innovation on Wall Street. "It's been a halcyon period in terms of taking financial innovation and using it to put housing much more deeply into the population," Ranieri proclaimed. "I mean, we've been able to franchise many, many more lower middle income and minority income individuals into home ownership, over the last four years, than probably in the 10 or 15 years prior to that."[15] The origins of mortgage securitization might have at least in part been motivated by a sense of social responsibility.

By the 2000s, however, Wall Street's craving for CMOs was based on a more simple appetite – originating, structuring, distributing, and then trading mortgage-backed securities had become the source of its greatest profits.

The business of securitizing mortgages had become so lucrative that some Wall Street firms even acquired lending institutions so as to assure a steady flow of deals and income. No longer content to act as a "middle man", Wall Street firms, became themselves "originators" of CMOs. This was a radical departure from the traditional investment banking business of helping others to issue and sell securities. Indeed, Wall Street was now in direct competition for loan origination business with the GSEs Fannie Mae and Freddie Mac.

As we shall see in Chapter five, Wall Street's foray into CMO origination was fraught with ethical conflicts and pitfalls that it had not even remotely considered before changing its business model. The scope, scale, and emphasis of principal transactions in mortgage securities on Wall Street can be gleaned from Lehman Brothers 2006 Annual Report (in words that one might imagine would seem wildly imprudent to a 1970s investment banker transported in time):

We originate residential and commercial mortgage loans as part of our mortgage trading and securitization activities and are a market leader in mortgage-backed securities trading. We securitized approximately $146 billion and $133 billion of residential mortgage loans in 2006 and 2005, respectively, including both originated loans and those we acquired in the secondary market. We originated approximately $60 billion and $85 billion of residential mortgage loans in 2006 and 2005, respectively. In addition, we originated approximately $34 billion and $27 billion of commercial mortgage loans in 2006 and 2005, respectively, the majority of which has been sold through securitization or syndication activities.[16]

By 2006, Wall Street was issuing more CMOs and providing financing for more mortgages than Fannie Mae or Freddie Mac. It was able to do so only by expanding the market into CMOs backed by subprime mortgages. Perverse compensation schemes further fueled Wall Street's obsession with CMOs. During the period from March 2007 through October 2008, seven financial firms – AIG, Bear Stearns, Countrywide, Lehman Brothers, Merrill Lynch, Wachovia, and Washington Mutual – went into bankruptcy, were taken over by the U.S. government, or were subsumed into the operations of larger solvent financial institutions. As detailed in Chapter three, a total of $493.2 million in bonuses was paid *in cash* over the two years prior to the financial crisis to the top five executives at these firms. Although the bonuses were paid in cash, the earnings and related asset valuations, particularly mortgage-backed securities valuations, that provided part of the basis for the compensation payments contained substantial ongoing economic risk. The average cash payment was more than $14 million with the largest two-year total paid to one executive exceeding $40 million. The risks became catastrophic losses when the CMO market collapsed. The full cash realization of the paper profits and the asset valuations that were the basis for the bonuses turned out to be fiction in the sense that substantial components of the reported earnings and asset values were never in fact actualized, meaning never realized in cash. Cash was never realized because certain business, accounting, and economic estimates and judgments that were used in the determination of reported earnings and asset valuations ultimately turned out to be wrong.

Conclusion: Financial Collapse and Moral Decay

Wall Street firms ended up stuck with substantial amounts of subprime securitized product in their inventories precisely at the time when the market began to understand and process the significance of the high default rates of subprime mortgages. Some firms like Goldman Sachs realized as early as December 2006 that it was time to get out, but virtually every other large financial institution with significant operations in the United States suffered massive losses from principal investments in subprime mortgages. Thanks to the repeal of the Glass-Steagall Act, no type of financial firm was spared. Traditional Wall Street institutions, new entrants into the securities business, and banking-insurance-securities conglomerates all eventually had to write-down the value of significant assets. Lehman Brothers bankruptcy in September 2008 accelerated the devaluation of the CMO market, but virtually every major U.S. financial institution was dangerously over-invested in the mortgage market. Indeed, as Figure 4.2 illustrates, Lehman's write downs actually were much smaller than those of many other institutions with larger capital bases. However in Lehman's case the losses wiped out its capital base (Figure 4.2).

The financial crisis was not simply an economic one. It was also a crisis in values. Wall Street's transformation into a trading leviathan was not accompanied by a correlative transformation of values. It became unmoored from its traditional concern for customers that dated back to the years just after the crash of 1929 when Charles Merrill and others restored public trust in the markets by putting the customer first. No new Wall Street values emerged to replace the old values. By 2000, the customer was no longer at the center of Wall Street's business model, and the client was no longer an essential moral

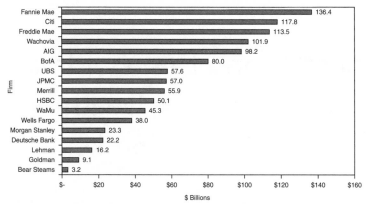

Figure 4.2. *Write-downs by financial institutions.*
Source: Schuermann, Til, Financial Market Stability and Systemic Risk, The Fed in the 21st Century, January 12, 2010; and Bloomberg.

concern for Wall Street executives. In fact, as we shall see in Chapter five, in the two years immediately preceding the financial crisis, the client became the "adversary" as Wall Street firms desperately struggled to survive by selling off their massive and risky bets on the mortgage market.

— ✤ **CHAPTER FIVE** ✤ —

Secrets and Lies: Goldman Sachs and the Death of the Honest Broker

Introduction

The turn of the millennium brought about radical change in the relationships of Wall Street firms with customers as well as to the broader economy and society – from clients to counterparties, from long-term relationships to transactional business, from guardians of efficient markets to exploiters of markets. In the postmillennial era, Wall Street firms exploit their expertise through proprietary principal transactions with counterparties whose interests are often in direct conflict with the firm. Transactions in which a firm's expertise is shared with clients have become less important to the bottom line.

Wall Street has, as a consequence, become less fit to fulfill its crucial free market roles of disseminating information about market value and serving as a vehicle for
the efficient allocation of capital.

Ironically, Wall Street in the postmillennial age pros-
pers by creating and exploiting inefficiencies in the free
market and not by helping it work efficiently. The new
Wall Street model requires firms to withhold information and analysis from those with whom they conduct
business. When the alignment of interests between Wall
Street firms and customers was severed so too was the
crucial link that enabled information to flow through
the financial markets. There were still functioning
financial markets that valued assets. However, particularly in relatively illiquid and opaque markets such as
that for mortgage-backed securities, the postmillennial
Wall Street model has embedded within it unprecedented incentives to lie and keep secrets from the market
in the hopes of gaining temporary profits from resulting informational asymmetries and inefficiencies. As a
result, Wall Street transactions sometimes obscure markets rather than provide information about them.

Goldman Sachs in 2007 epitomized the business model
and mores of postmillennial Wall Street. In 2007 Goldman
Sachs made billions of dollars, whereas the counterparties
it did business with lost billions. It had the most profitable

year in its history just as the global economy was heading into a tailspin. We focus in particular on the activities of Goldman Sachs over a discrete and crucial period of time: the desperate months from December 2006, when the firm came to the collective realization that it was dangerously overinvested in mortgage-related securities, to May 2007 by which time the firm had successfully unwound its long position and adopted a short position that would prove to be hugely profitable. Goldman's plan to convert losses into profits required secrecy and deception about its valuation of mortgage-backed securities. The less information its clients and the market in general knew about the firm's evaluation of the true state of the market, the better off Goldman Sachs would be. It needed to conduct trading activities without providing information to the market – something it was able to accomplish through secrets and lies. The crucial link between Wall Street and clients was severed at the precise point in time when the financial markets needed information to flow most efficiently. Goldman saved itself in the first half of 2007, but it did so by using deceptive methods and helping prolong inefficiencies in the valuation of mortgage-related securities, all ultimately increasing the taxpayer cost of the bailout.

In scrutinizing Goldman Sachs during this approximately six-month time frame we will highlight ethical issues arising in the various transactions with customers – for instance, the Abacus deal made infamous by Senator Carl Levin in 2010 hearings. Abacus was part of the firm's swift and nimble shift from a massive exposure to subprime mortgages to a substantial net short position. It was intuitively troubling for many to learn that in early 2007 Goldman Sachs was originating CDOs (Collateralized Debt Obligations) based on residential mortgage payments and selling them to purchasers at the exact same time that the firm was urgently unloading similar securities from their own capital account. Disturbing too was the revelation that the mortgages referenced in the Abacus deal were specifically chosen to have a high risk of failing. It was this intuitive understanding that led Senator Levin to declare: "the evidence shows that Goldman repeatedly put its own interests and profits ahead of the interests of its clients."[1] We are interested, however, not only in the ethics of the relationships between Goldman Sachs and its clients. We are also concerned about the economic and moral consequences of Goldman Sachs's client deception on the broader capital markets.

Goldman Sachs was by no means the only firm engaging in deceptive business practices devoid of respect for clients. Citigroup, Deutsche Bank, JPMorgan Chase, Morgan Stanley, and Merrill Lynch all either settled a government or private action charging fraud or were the subject of congressional investigation. Although Goldman Sachs's practices are our primary focus, we discuss these other firms as well. When these cases are taken together, the composite profile that emerges paints a disturbing picture of postmillennial Wall Street values in decay and decline.

Goldman Sachs in 2007: A Year for the Ages

Goldman Sachs had a banner year in 2007, a year for the ages. It earned $17.6 billion pretax dollars on revenues of $46 billion. What made the firm's 2007 performance even more remarkable was that poor risk control practices and massive exposure to the collapsing CDO market made the year an *annus horribilis* for other Wall Street firms. Merrill Lynch had $8 billion in losses, reversing a $7 billion gain from the previous year, and Citibank's profits declined over 80 percent in 2007. By March 2008 Bear Stearns would nearly go out of business and be sold off. Lehman Brothers' bankruptcy filing a few months later would trigger a global financial crisis. There were, to be sure, some big winners among all the carnage. Goldman Sachs was unique, however, because the winners were mostly loner hedge fund managers who early in 2006 sharpened their pencils and technical analysis and began to see the mortgage bubble for what it was.

These managers included Steve Eisman and Mike Burry, both profiled in Michael Lewis's *The Big Short*, and billionaire John Paulson whom Gregory Zuckerman lionized in *The Greatest Trade Ever*.[2] These were the truly visionary investors who saw through the triple-A ratings and the hype around mortgage-backed securities and placed huge winning bets by shorting the market. In fact, the only reason these hedge fund managers could not make even more money was because, as Michael Lewis writes in *The Big Short*, large and established Wall Street firms thought they were too small and too inconsequential to be allowed to place larger short positions.

Goldman Sachs did not make billions of dollars in 2007 because it had smart and visionary traders and technical analysts who computed the numbers like their iconoclastic counterparts in the hedge fund world. The firm's path to record profits was a steady organizational triumph rather than one of clever individual trading prowess. Even as late as December 2006 the firm was so over-invested in CDOs that, had it not immediately reversed course completely, the firm may well have followed Bear Stearns and Lehman Brothers into insolvency. What saved the firm was its ability to detect, quickly process, and nimbly adjust to market signals and looming economic realities. The time frame becomes crucial here in understanding both Goldman's achievement in making such huge profits and the deception, lies, and secrets it employed to do so. By the summer of 2006, iconoclastic hedge fund shorts such as John Paulson and Steve Eisman were convinced that the mortgage-backed securities market would collapse once the financial markets understood and processed high rates of defaults already occurring among subprime mortgages. Goldman Sachs was executing short trades for Paulson & Co., the hedge fund managed by John Paulson. Paulson's short trades alerted the firm to the fact that something might be wrong with its own long positions. To Goldman Sachs's credit it heard and acted upon these market signals when other firms were blithely ignoring them and plunging ever deeper into the abyss.

December 14, 2006: Goldman Tacks 180 Degrees into the Wind

On December 14, 2006, David Viniar, the chief financial officer of Goldman Sachs, presided over a meeting attended by, among others, the senior management of the firm's mortgage department. Throughout 2006, various business units within the department held conflicting views of the future direction of the MBS market. By December, according to a 2011 United States Senate Report (the Senate Report) Goldman Sachs was holding $6

billion of inventory in CDOs, much of that in
Despite the firm's long position in CDOs, many w
mortgage department had become decidedly bea
mid-2006, the Senate Report notes, the departme
a "predominantly pessimistic" view of the U.S. sub
mortgage market. Michael Swenson, head of the
gage department's Structured Products Group told Se
investigators that "during the early summer of 200
was clear that the market fundamentals in subprime a
the highly levered nature of CDOs [were] going to have
very unhappy ending."[4] Through the fall of 2006, Vinia
and others in the firm's executive management became
increasingly concerned about the firm's $6 billion expo-
sure to the CDO market. At the December 14 meeting
the decision was made to reduce, and if possible elimi-
nate entirely, the firm's exposure, with particular emphasis on shedding subprime mortgage products held in its
inventory. It would be three to six months before other
Wall Street firms fully understood the magnitude of their
miscalculation about the mortgage market. When these
other firms did come to the realization, it was too late to
avoid the massive losses that they would suffer in 2007.
Goldman Sachs, however, figured out the market just in
time and shifted nimbly to turn crisis into opportunity.

Goldman Sachs had a number of distinctive organizational strengths enabling it to assimilate market

information quickly, reverse course adroitly, and thereby turn potentially devastating losses into record-setting gains. First and foremost, as exemplified by the December 14 meeting, was a corporate culture enabling the firm to collaboratively assess and respond quickly and effectively to changing market conditions. The firm also had a strong and well-integrated risk management system that required a daily reckoning of market value and risk, served as a check on the firm's traders, and imposed enterprise-wide discipline on the firm's investments. Goldman's organizational strengths stood in sharp contrast to the management practices of firms like Merrill Lynch where risk management officers were marginalized from the trading operations and where CEO Stanley O'Neal believed, as late as September 2007, that the firm stood to lose less than $100 million, when in fact the losses would eventually amount to over $55 billion and require the firm to be sold off to Bank of America in a hastily arranged fire sale.[5]

In the months following the December 14 meeting, Goldman Sachs executed a coordinated trio of tactics to move from dangerous exposure to the subprime market to a banner year of profits.[6] First, Goldman Sachs traders sold off as much as they could of the $6 billion in CDOs the firm held in its own proprietary accounts. Second, the firm sought ways to hedge its existing inventory, including buying as much "insurance" or CDSs as AIG

was foolish enough to write. Third, as Goldman Sachs went about shedding its inventory of MBS and aggressively taking short positions, it continued to earn fees through new MBS offerings. It was this last tactic that drew heavy scrutiny from Senate investigators. In spite of having made the decision on December 14, 2006, to reduce the firm's exposure to the mortgage market, Goldman Sachs continued to originate, structure, and sell mortgage products to customers. As highlighted in the report of the U.S. Senate Permanent Subcommittee on Investigations, "the Goldman Sachs case study focuses on how it used net short positions to benefit from the downturn in the mortgage market, and designed, marketed, and sold CDOs in ways that created conflicts of interest with the firm's clients and at times led to the bank's profiting from the same products that caused substantial losses for its clients."[7]

After the December 14 meeting, Goldman Sachs did not use its collective judgment about the direction of the market to help clients navigate out of the disaster CDO investments would become. To the contrary, the firm implemented a ruthless and coordinated business strategy across all its business units that benefited the firm at the expense of clients. To save itself, Goldman Sachs hid its true opinion from its customers. To successfully implement its U-turn on CDOs, the firm had to stretch and, in some cases, overstep legal and ethical boundaries about when information should be shared with clients, counterparties, and the market as a whole.

It would be unjust to condemn Goldman Sachs merely for being a winner, that is, for correctly assessing the economic realities of the housing market and the true value of CDOs. Some might even argue that short trading by Goldman Sachs provided the capital markets with an important signal of underlying problems, and that the free market system was simply working the way it was supposed to work to create overall social efficiency. By sorting out the winners and losers on the short and long side of the market, the housing market would be steered back from its bubble highs to values more closely reflecting underlying fundamentals. When we take a more granular look at Goldman Sachs's actions in the first desperate months of 2007, however, what we see is far from a compelling advertisement for the virtues of the free market. What we witnessed was the decay and decline of postmillennial Wall Street values. To save itself, Goldman Sachs employed secrets, and lies. It intentionally created misleading information. It touted the financial benefits of investing in CDOs to customers even as it was secretly unloading all that it could from its own inventory. It went through great lengths to hide the fact that it was short in the market and even short in the very transactions it was selling to clients. In lying to and deceiving its clients, it acted outside the ethical and legal bounds of the free market. Moreover, the transactions initiated by Goldman Sachs early in 2007 were not trades of existing CDOs providing information about the firm's view of the market. Indeed, they were not even technically "trades" although they were brought to market by the firm's mortgage trading unit. In fact, they were newly created CDOs sold to clients accompanied by what appeared to be traditional offering memoranda. This gave clients the false impression that the deals were vetted by Goldman Sachs acting as a traditional honest broker underwriter, whereas in fact they were specifically designed to stealthily enable Goldman Sachs to sell out its long position in CDOs and establish a massive short position. These transactions in the first desperate months of 2007 thus had the net effect of creating market disinformation rather than market information. As a result, the firm's success contributed to the growth of the overall market's exposure to subprime risk.

Decaying Wall Street Values: The Demise of the Honest Broker

In previous chapters, we described how the rise of proprietary trading transformed the postmillennial Wall

Street business model from symbiotic dependency and mutual profitability with clients to a beggar thy neighbor model in which the interests of Wall Street firms directly conflicted with the counterparties with whom they did business. A related transformation occurred when Wall Street firms themselves became originators or issuers of CDOs, and compromised their role as "honest brokers" in the securities markets.

The so-called dot com boom and bust of the early 2000s presaged the unhinging of the essential Wall Street value of being an honest broker rather than an interested principal in transactions with clients. Up to that point, it had been considered an essential skill for investment bankers to price IPOs correctly – that is, the trading value of the stock would not vary too much on the high side (thereby shortchanging the issuer in the amount of funds to be raised) or the low side (thereby causing immediate losses to investors). The art and science of investment banking lay in making the right valuation of the issuing company's worth. The investment banker in the underwriting process had to serve as an honest broker between issuers and investors. It was crucial to the business model of every Wall Street firm to be trusted by both sides in the underwriting process.[8] During the dot com boom, however, many Wall Street firms promoted IPOs of start-up companies with short track records and dubious prospects. They priced those securities well below the red hot aftermarket for them, and made substantial profits (far more than they earned in traditional underwriting fees in some cases) by buying and selling those hot issues for their own proprietary accounts and by allocating such profits to favored customers – including executives of firms with whom they did or hoped to do business.[9] The dot com bust whittled away at traditional honest broker Wall Street values. The subprime mortgage business took a sledgehammer to those values.

Acting as securities originators or issuers during the mortgage bubble represented a radical departure from the role traditionally played by Wall Street firms as underwriters of securities – that is, as intermediaries or honest brokers between issuers and investors. Under the traditional business model where the firms acted as underwriters, investment banks were jointly and severally liable (with issuers) for errors and omissions in disclosure to investors, thereby creating powerful incentives to help assure that information available to investors was complete and accurate. This was a particularly powerful incentive in the days when the investment firms were organized as partnerships. Wall Street, however, had long sought to increase profits by reaching deeper into the supply chain of mortgage origination.[10] Some firms even extended their reach to the point where mortgages were created by purchasing mortgage origination businesses, as for example when Merrill Lynch acquired First Franklin Financial Corporation in December 2006. Goldman Sachs did not go as deeply into the supply chain as other Wall Street firms but it did expand its business line by originating, packaging, and selling CDOs. As noted in the Senate Report: "In its mortgage business, Goldman Sachs acted as a market maker, underwriter, placement agent, and proprietary trader in residential and commercial mortgage related securities, loan products, and other asset backed and derivative products."[11]

An examination of Goldman Sachs's organizational structure helps elucidate how radical a departure CDO issuance was from the traditional Wall Street business model. In 2007 Goldman had three basic business divisions: (1) Investment Banking, (2) Trading and Principal Investments, and (3) Asset Management and Securities Services (Figure 5.1). Trading and Principal Investments was further organized into three distinct groups, each with separate management: (1) Fixed Income, Currency, and Commodities (FICC); (2) Equities; and (3) Principal Investments.[12] The FICC group housed the mortgage department and related businesses. The mortgage department had complete operating responsibility for Goldman's mortgage business activities, including

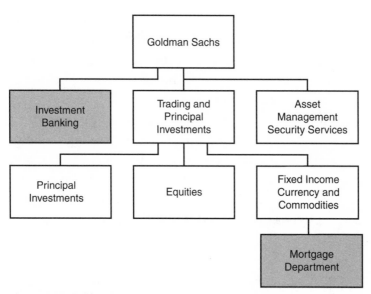

Figure 5.1. *Goldman Sachs 2007 business organization chart.*
Source: 2011 Senate Report.

originating, structuring, marketing, and selling mortgage-backed products such as CDOs and related CDSs. All
other transactions in which the firm acted as underwriter
were managed through the Investment Banking division
where the professional staff worried about keeping clients happy and acting as an honest broker between issuers and investors. In the CDO business, Goldman Sachs
was conducting underwriting *of its own issuer securities* and
selling those securities to clients *in the same department*

that was responsible for the firm's proprietary trading profits in CDOs. Traders, in other words, were conducting or supervising the traditional underwriting job done by investment bankers for deals they themselves were creating and promoting. However, these traders did not have the same Wall Street values as traditional investment bankers, values instilled and nurtured through symbiotic relationships with clients that were institutional and long-standing. These relationships even spanned generations of bankers and clients. It is little wonder that traders who were not trained in this tradition put together deals fraught with hidden dangers for investors. In 2007, as Goldman was desperately trying to reverse its long position in CDO, the temptation to unload their inventory made every customer who did CDO-related business with Goldman Sachs potential prey for abuse.

The Desperate Months: Secrets and Lies

A closer look at four transactions originated and sold to clients by Goldman Sachs during the desperate months from December 2006 through April 2007 exemplifies Wall Street's abandonment of its role as an honest broker.

The Hudson I and II CDOs were conceived during the summer of 2006 when some of the executives in the mortgage department observed the firm's hedge fund client John Paulson making ever-larger trades on the short side of the mortgage market and determined the firm should begin to initiate transactions of the short side for its own accounts.[13] The firm started marketing the Hudson CDOs – backed by residential mortgage-backed securities (RMBS) – in October. Hudson I sales commenced on December 5, 2006, and sales in Hudson II commenced on February 8, 2007. The design and structure of the Hudson CDOs constituted an exquisitely timed first step in the implementation of CFO David Viniar's December 14 decision to reverse the course of the entire firm on the mortgage market. The Hudson offering was a hybrid structure. The mortgage exposure for investors comprised a CDO based partly on real-world mortgage loans originated to finance home ownership and partly on derivative contract credit default swaps (CDSs) that made reference to pools of existing mortgages. Goldman Sachs provided the real-world mortgages and also was the party to the CDS in the derivative part of the deal. The net economic effect of the Hudson CDS was casino capitalism at its zenith – Goldman Sachs was betting that the value of the mortgage-backed CDS would go down, and its customers or "counterparties" were betting it would go up. Once originated, a CDO trades in the secondary market and the price of the CDO reflects prevailing information about the main factors that generally influence price – for instance, credit risk, interest rate risk, and systemic risk. The price of the CDO will fluctuate, and if default rates on the underlying mortgages increase, the price of the CDO will decline. Within a very few months Goldman Sachs's bet paid off in spectacular fashion. The Hudson I deal alone enabled the firm to reduce its inventory of CDOs by $800 million and also to create a short position through CDSs valued at $1.2 billion. As summarized by the Senate Committee report:

In the case of Hudson I, for example, Goldman took 100% of the short side of the $2 billion CDO, betting against the assets referenced in the CDO, and sold the Hudson securities to investors without disclosing its short position. When the securities lost value, Goldman made a $1.7 billion gain at the direct expense of the clients to whom it had sold the securities.[14]

Timberwolf I was a $1 billion hybrid transaction that came to market in early 2007. The value of the Timberwolf I CDOs began declining almost as soon as customers purchased them. In fact, Goldman Sachs sold the securities to its clients at prices that were higher than the firm was valuing the securities in its own accounts at the time of the sale. Adding insult to injury, Goldman Sachs loaned its "clients" the funds to purchase the securities, and after it marked the securities down to their real value within weeks after the sale, Goldman Sachs required the "clients" to pay cash immediately to secure the loan! The only problem from the firm's point of view was that the CDO market was moving down so fast in the first desperate months of 2007 that it could not unload all the Timberwolf CDOs quickly enough. Within five months of being issued, the securities lost 80 percent of their value, and the firm got caught holding a large portion of them. Nevertheless, overall Goldman Sachs made substantial profits by taking 36 percent of the CDS's short position.[15]

Anderson Mezzanine 2007–1 closed on March 20, 2007. Lenders such as New Century, Fremont, and Countrywide originated the mortgages referenced in these synthetic securities. These were subprime lenders known within the industry for issuing poor quality loans.[16] The U.S. Senate report notes that "during the same time period in which the Anderson single name credit default swap contracts were being accumulated, Goldman was becoming increasingly concerned about the subprime mortgage market, was reacting to bad news from the subprime lenders it did business with, and *was building a large short position against the same types of ... securities referenced in Anderson*" (emphasis added). In other words, Goldman Sachs was selling its clients the precise kinds of securities that it was betting against with its own capital. The Senate Report continues with a disturbing description of the lengths to which Goldman Sachs went to deceive clients about the firm's own trading posture and judgment about the market value of the referenced securities:

> When a client asked how Goldman "got comfortable" with the New Century loans in the CDS, Goldman personnel tried to dispel concerns about the loans, and did not disclose the firm's own negative view of them or its short position in the CDO ... essentially betting against the very securities it was selling to its clients. Instead, Goldman instructed its sales force to tell potential investors that Goldman was buying up to 50% of the equity tranche. Goldman also did not disclose to potential investors that it had almost cancelled the CDO due to the falling value of its assets.[17]

The Anderson deal epitomizes Goldman Sachs's disdainful attitude toward clients. The transaction not only involved the deliberate sale of a security that would almost certainly lose value, but also showed a complete lack of forthrightness about the firm's true market judgment. In an earlier era, it would have been unthinkable for a Wall Street professional to take an enormously large position with its own capital and advise its client to take a diametrically opposite position while withholding its best market judgment from the client.

The now infamous Abacus 2007 AC-1 deal closed on April 26, 2007, by which time Goldman Sachs had completed its goal of converting its exposure to mortgage risk from the long side to the short side. A significant feature of Abacus 2007 was that, unbeknownst to the customers, an external hedge fund, Paulson & Co., was the CDS counterparty to their investment. The Abacus CDSs referenced specific BBB-rated mortgage pools issued in 2006 and early 2007 that were handpicked by Paulson as being among the most likely to fail.[18] Goldman's salespeople then undertook to sell $2 billion of this "suckers' bet" to its customers without disclosing Paulson's role. Goldman Sachs was in essence renting its then still good name for a $15 million fee. In its lawsuit accusing Goldman Sachs of securities fraud, the SEC alleged that the firm "failed to disclose to investors vital information about the CDO, in particular the role that a major hedge fund played in the portfolio selection process and the fact that the hedge fund had taken a short position against the CDO."[19] According to the SEC, "83 percent of the Abacus portfolio had been downgraded by Oct. 24, 2007, and 17 percent was on negative watch. By Jan. 29, 2008, 99 percent of the portfolio had been downgraded." Investors in Abacus CDOs lost more than $1 billion. According to the Senate Report, Goldman also failed to disclose Paulson & Co.'s role to the credit rating agency that assigned AAA ratings to the two tranches of Abacus securities. Although many questions have been and continue to be raised regarding the Abacus transaction, the most disquieting one may be why Goldman

Sachs would trade the firm's decades-in-the-making reputation for integrity and honest dealing for a mere $15 million in fees.

The Death of the Client: A Desperate Wall Street Unloads Toxic Assets on Clients in 2007

Goldman Sachs was not alone in destroying the fundamental client-centered values that had sustained Wall street and the financial systmen for more than a half-century. As we have described in preceding chapters, the death of the client on Wall Street had been in process for over two decades – dating back to the Salomon Brothers, Merrill Lynch, and Bankers Trust scandals of the 1980s. In 2007, as market conditions worsened, the ashes of the client-centered financial services industry were scattered unceremoniously all over Wall Street as firms desperately endeavored to survive by originating and selling deliberately flawed CDOs to clients.

Even financial firms that were huge overall losers in the mortgage CDO sector, including Citicorp and JPMorgan Chase, desperately attempted to mitigate their losses by using secrets and lies to unload their toxic asset inventories on unsuspecting clients. What united all these transactions is that they sought to profit from deliberately created informational asymmetries based upon deceptions. In a radical departure from traditional Wall Street values, firms did not share expertise, knowledge, and judgment with clients. Rather, clients were viewed as counterparties to be duped and kept in relative ignorance.

The same Senate committee that examined Goldman Sachs also investigated the CDO activities of Deutsche Bank. The Senate report concluded that Deutsche Bank also originated, structured, and sold CDOs to the market at a time when its CDO mortgage traders strongly believed that the value of these securities would decline substantially.[20] In describing one deal, the Committee noted:

> Nearly a third of the RMBS securities contained subprime loans originated by Fremont, Long Beach, and New Century, lenders well known within the industry for issuing poor quality loans. Deutsche Bank also sold securities directly from its own inventory to the CDO. Deutsche Bank's CDO trading desk knew that many of these RMBS securities were likely to lose value, but did not object to their inclusion.[21]

In 2011, the SEC signed settlement agreements with JPMorgan Chase and Citicorp. The SEC had charged JPMorgan Chase with misleading investors in a mortgage security transaction completed just as the housing market was starting to plummet. JPMorgan Chase agreed to pay \$153.6 million to investors.[22] The SEC charged Citicorp with misleading its clients in a \$1 billion CDO. Citicorp agreed to settle the case by paying \$285 million to clients.[23] More such civil enforcement actions are likely, as the SEC has subpoenaed documents from Morgan Stanley, UBS, and Deutsche Bank, among other firms, in connection with transactions in the years immediately preceding the financial crisis.[24]

It would be remiss to survey the various deceptive and fraudulent methods Wall Street firms employed to obscure and distort the capital market's valuation of mortgage-related securities without mentioning Lehman Brothers, the firm whose bankruptcy in September 2008 was the veritable Fort Sumter of the financial crisis. Goldman Sachs engaged in deceptive practices to achieve record profits. Citicorp and JPMorgan Chase did so to cut their losses. Lehman Brothers manipulated corporate accounting and financial reporting to delay public knowledge of its insolvency. In each case the economic end result was the same – the intentional obfuscation of information in the capital markets which had the net effect of prolonging the grossly mistaken valuation of the mortgage market. All of these practices wound up increasing the cost of the government bailout and seriously damaging the country's long-term prospects for innovation and job growth.

Lehman Brothers filed for bankruptcy on Monday, September 15, 2008. It was the largest bankruptcy in the history of the United States – larger than WorldCom, larger than Enron. Just a few months prior to declaring bankruptcy, Lehman was the fourth largest broker/dealer in the United States, having declared record profits in 2007. Astonishingly, on September 10, 2008, *a mere 5 days prior to the bankruptcy filing*, Lehman disseminated preliminary third quarter 2008 financial statements claiming shareholders' equity of over $28 billion.[25]

The bankruptcy receiver, Anton R. Valukas, chairman of the law firm Jenner & Block and a former federal prosecutor, reported that Lehman Brothers employed highly questionable "Repo 105" accounting to cosmetically remove selected assets and liabilities from the balance sheet.[26] By temporarily reducing liabilities, the firm deceived regulators and investors about its true leverage ratio – the amount of borrowing relative to assets. Mr. Valukas characterized these accounting practices as "materially misleading." By accounting sleight of hand, Lehman Brothers managed to shuffle billions off its books in the months before its collapse in September 2008, thereby concealing the full extent of its borrowings and leverage ratio. According to Mr. Valukas, senior Lehman Brothers executives, as well as the bank's public accountants, were aware of these deceptive practices.[27]

Legal and Ethical Principles for Evaluating Wall Street's Behavior in 2007

What legal and ethical principles should be applied to judge Wall Street's mistreatment of clients in the desperate first months of 2007? To date, the government has engaged in an unfortunate pattern of settling lawsuits with Wall Street firms without determining the legal status of their actions. Private law suits brought by financially injured clients offer another potential means of establishing clear lines of legal responsibility. However, it will take some years before these cases wind their way through the trial and appellate systems, and it is far from certain that they will result in a coherent set of consistent and clearly delineated principles. Despite the absence to date of legal certainty, it is possible to point to a number of factors relevant to drawing the line between responsible behavior from behavior that violates fundamental ethical and legal principles of fairness and justice. One critical factor is timing. From the Senate Report we know that on December 14, 2006, Goldman Sachs made a firm-wide decision to reverse course and go short on the mortgage market. This date forms a very clear line of demarcation. CDO transactions sold before are in a different ethical and legal realm than those sold after. Before this date Goldman

Sachs as a firm was either decidedly bullish on about the CDO market or, as 2006 unfolded, in a position of equipoise. Some individuals and business units within the firm believed that the mortgage market would move in a positive direction. Others believed the opposite or had no definite opinion. The firm as a whole was $6 billion long in mortgage-related securies. As a consequence, CDO transactions completed before December 14, 2006, do not, absent other factors constituting fraud, generate ethical concerns, even if the value of the investment declined, and even if Goldman Sachs profited from the short side. CDOs sold after the December 14, 2006 Viniar meeting fall into a different legal and ethical category.

In each case we examined – Hudson, Timberwolf, Anderson, and Abacus – Goldman Sachs sold the CDOs after forming a strong firm-wide judgment that the CDO market was in serious trouble and while the firm was investing its own capital against the advice it was giving to clients. Other firms, such as Citicorp and JPMorgan Chase, also evolved from a bullish view or genuinely uncertain market judgment to an unambiguously negative view, although these firms completed this process some months after Goldman Sachs. The specific date that these firms decisively shifted to a negative firm-wide judgment of the CDO market, if it can be ascertained, also has legal and moral significance.

The question of timing has proven to be relevant in the divergent results of a pair of private civil cases for monetary damages. In the *Dodona* case a federal district court ruled that facts alleged by Dodona I, an institutional investor, in connection with the Hudson transaction would (if proven) be sufficient to establish fraud because the sale occurred after December 14, 2006.[28] In the *Landesbanke* case, a German bank also accused Goldman Sachs of fraud, alleging that the firm knew that the underlying mortgages were riskier than described in the offering circular. However, the *Landesbanke* court dismissed the complaint because there was no evidence that "Goldman knew in March of 2006 about the toxicity of the mortgages."[29]

Besides timing, other factors are relevant to the legal and ethical evaluation of the CDO deals Wall Street churned out in 2007. To wit: (1) whether the informational asymmetry concerned facts or opinions (As a legal matter, to establish fraud, it is necessary to show that a fact has been misrepresented; possessing a different opinion about the worth of something being sold has no bearing on the validity or fairness of the contract.); (2) whether that information was merely withheld or deliberately misrepresented; and (3) whether the nature of the relationship between the parties created any special duty of candor.

When applied to the four transactions we have examined from the desperate months of 2007, these criteria raise a number of questions. Did Goldman Sachs have a duty to disclose its decidedly negative opinion about the CDO market to its customers? Did it have a duty to disclose that it was the on the short side of the credit default swaps that were part of the CDO offering? Did the firm merely withhold its opinion or did it misrepresent its judgment? In the Abacus deal, did it have a duty to disclose that the hedge fund led by John Paulson deliberately selected a mortgage portfolio with a high chance of failing? Does it matter that the purchasers of the CDOs were "sophisticated" institutional investors to whom the firm owed no fiduciary duties?

In its own defense, Goldman Sachs, during the Senate Committee hearings, asserted that it was only responding to unsolicited purchase inquiries, also known as "reverse inquiries" in the securities business.[30] However, after extensive interviews and reviews of documents and emails, the Senate Committee concluded: "Under its CDO Game plan, Goldman 'targeted' four primary and 35 secondary clients for CDO sales, and celebrated selling CDO securities to several of them. The weight of this evidence demonstrates that Goldman was soliciting sales rather than responding solely to client inquiries."[31] The firm has also asserted a *caveat emptor* defense, insisting that it has no particular duty – fiduciary or otherwise – to disclose any of these facts and opinions to the kinds of sophisticated institutional investors who purchased the CDOs. The firm's lawyers also have argued that the informational circulars distributed to investors clearly labeled the investments as "speculative" and warned of the risky nature of investing in securities, the possibility of market downturns, and the risks generally associated with mortgage-backed assets. Moreover, as a legal matter, the firm is not a fiduciary or investment adviser to the clients who purchased the CDOs. It certainly cannot be said to owe fiduciary duties to another Wall Street icon, Morgan Stanley, which lost $960 million on Hudson CDOs.

Notwithstanding the fact that the CDOs were sold to sophisticated investors, the ethical and legal problem for Goldman Sachs is that it did not merely fail to disclose an opinion about the state of the CDO market. For example, the marketing materials presented to potential investors in the Hudson offering described the CDOs as "a consistent, programmatic approach to invest in attractive relative value opportunities in the RMBS and structured product markets."[32] The firm thus did not simply decline to offer its opinion. It affirmatively and inaccurately represented the risk of investing in the Hudson CDOs. Neither as a matter of law nor ethics is this kind of affirmative misrepresentation excused by the fact that the

Secrets and Lies

sales materials contained general boilerplate disclaimers. That is because those disclaimers are themselves deceptive in that they knowingly and deliberately misrepresent Goldman Sachs's true assessment of the risks of the transaction.

Time and again, Goldman followed the same pattern of deliberate deception. In the Abacus case, the SEC charged that Goldman Sachs employee Fabrice Tourre wrote emails to potential clients extolling the virtues of the CDOs he was pushing, while at the same time failing to disclose John Paulson's role in putting together a portfolio of mortgages deliberately designed to lose value.[33] In the Hudson deal, the firm disclosed in one part of the sales materials that an affiliated entity was the "sole credit protection buyer," in essence revealing that it was on the short side of the credit default swaps being purchased by its customers. However, elsewhere the sales materials claimed that "Goldman has aligned incentives with the Hudson program by investing in a portion of equity,"[34] thereby deliberately trying to create the misleading impression that the CDO investment was not as risky as Goldman Sachs actually believed it to be. This pattern of intentional misrepresentation and deception dances right up against and falls over the line of what is legally and ethically acceptable behavior. As Judge Victor Marrero wrote in the *Dodona* case: "an incomplete or misleading disclosure may be just as damaging as total concealment."[35]

Structural Reform and Effective Management of Conflict of Interest

As we have seen, Goldman Sachs, as did other firms acting as originators of subprime CDOs and selling them to investors, still went through the legal niceties associated with traditional underwritings. They provided investors with information prospectuses that had the superficial appearance of a traditional private placement in which the underwriter plays an intermediary role between issuer and investor and vets the truthfulness of the statements. The lawyers and accountants for Goldman Sachs and other investment banks even cleverly made sure that the statements of risk appearing in the prospectuses had the same kinds of warnings and disclaimers that might have been included if there actually were an independent underwriter. However, investors and the market in general for CDOs were deprived of the genuine and healthy skepticism that ensues when underwriters are independent of issuers and are jointly liable for their misstatements and omissions. Instead of acting as honest brokers between issuers and investors (with a client relationship to both parties), Wall Street firms became direct sellers to investors. The honest broker became a casualty of postmillennial Wall Street. As Judge Sidney H. Stein observed in a case brought by disgruntled shareholders, "Citigroup, as the underwriter of the CDOs it held, knew the inputs and assumptions that went into creating these assets and thus was in the best position to recognize the threats they faced as the subprime mortgage market deteriorated."[36] This problem was exacerbated at Goldman Sachs in particular by the fact that the offering materials for newly created CDO debt securities were being prepared within a trading unit that had neither the technical expertise nor the investment banking mind-set to perform the traditional due diligence role of checking the truthfulness of claims in the sales materials.

After the Senate Committee hearing, but prior to both the final Senate Committee report and to a $550 million settlement with the SEC, Goldman Sachs issued a *Report of the Business Standards Committee*. The avowed purpose of the report, issued in January 2011 was to present the results of a "comprehensive" review of the firm's business practices and standards in light of the financial crisis. The report is replete with self-serving platitudes including some reaching Orwellian levels of disingenuousness. "Our clients' interests always come first," the report proclaims. "Our experience shows that if we serve our clients well, our own success will follow."[37] One obscure passage in the report does, however, obliquely reveal that the firm's pre-crisis business practices fell well short of Goldman Sachs's own ethical standards:

The Business Standards Committee recommends that certain underwriting and origination activities be moved from the Securities Division to the Financing Group within IBD [Investment Banking Division], including certain activities related to mortgage-backed and asset-backed securitization, emerging markets debt and money market instruments such as commercial paper. Business units of the Securities Division that continue to conduct origination activities will have policies and standards, approval processes, disclosure requirements and oversight that are consistent with those that apply to all origination activities in IBD. This recommendation reflects our objectives of strengthening client relationships and reputational excellence.[38]

This little noticed recommendation is a tacit admission by Goldman Sachs that its CDO origination business should not have been conducted in the same business unit responsible for trading CDOs with the firm's own capital. More fundamentally, it is an acknowledgment that the firm, by design, did not rigorously fulfill its underwriter duty of due diligence owed to clients. By moving securities origination activities into the investment banking division, the firm was essentially admitting that the "policies and standards, approval processes, disclosure requirements, and oversight" of transactions conducted in the first desperate months of 2007 fell short of the firm's ethical obligations to clients.

Had Goldman Sachs acted as the truly independent underwriter in the Anderson CDO deal would this deal have come to market? If Brand X Company tried to hire Goldman Sachs as an independent underwriter for the Abacus deal, would the firm's due diligence have failed to uncover that John Paulson handpicked the portfolio to fail? Would Goldman Sachs have allowed that deal to be sold to its clients without making sure that they were made aware of this fact? The answer to all these questions is quite obviously no. Will it make a difference now that Goldman Sachs has moved responsibility for its origination to the Financing Group? What difference will this reorganization make in its standard of candor, due diligence, and honest dealing with clients? Will the traditional Wall Street values of investment banking – acting as an honest broker between the issuer and purchaser of securities – prevail? Or will there be overwhelming pressure on investment bankers to adapt their business practices and values to suit the firm's principal transaction business model? Only time and experience will be able to answer these questions.

Conclusion: Toward Sustainable
Wall Street Values

Goldman Sachs has the well-deserved reputation for employing some of the best and the brightest minds on Wall Street. Yet at the precise moment when clients, customers, the markets, and the public were most in need of clear and accurate information about the mortgage market, the bright minds at Goldman Sachs best positioned to provide that information were engaged in an elaborate charade of deception that fell below ethical standards (Table 5.1). As the lawsuits against Goldman Sachs proceed in the courts, time will tell whether their actions also fell below legal standards. The firm, in essence, saved itself by misleading its clients and impeding the information flow needed for the efficient functioning of free markets. It helped prolong the valuation bubble in mortgage-related securities and ultimately added to the financial and human costs of the financial crisis. Rarely has the moral disjunction between corporate profits and public welfare been as great as it was between Goldman Sachs and the public welfare in the first half of 2007.

Also troubling is the manner in which Goldman Sachs has gone about trying to defend its actions. Former SEC Chairman Richard C. Breeden famously remarked after

Table 5.1. *Goldman Sachs: Timeline*

> Summer 2006: John Paulson, Steve Eisman accumulating positions (*The Big Short*)
> July 10, 2006: Henry Paulson joins Treasury Department
> December 2006: Goldman Sachs $6 billion long in mortgage-related securities
> December 14, 2006: David Viniar meets with Mortgage Department – Decision is made to reverse course on MBS
> December 2006–April 2007-Goldman markets Hudson, Abacus, Timberwolf and Anderson deals to customers
> June 2007: Goldman Sachs $13.9 billion short
> June 2007: Starts marking down CDOs (Increases the value of Goldman's net short position, while lowering the value of CDOs held by many customers. As a consequence of the arrangement made to finance the CDO holdings, some Goldman clients had to post additional collateral due to the lower valuations

---

Source: 2011 Senate Report; W. Cohan, *Money and Power* (2011); M. Lewis, *The Big Short* (2010).

the Salomon Brothers treasury securities scandal in 1991 "it is not an adequate ethical standard to aspire to get through the day without being indicted." These words ring ever true as we look back to the events leading to the 2008 financial crisis. As the many and sundry government and private lawsuits against Goldman Sachs and other Wall Street firms are fiercely litigated in the courts, we must not forget the crucial difference between the minimum ethical standards that determine legal liability and the kinds of values and higher ethical principles that are needed to establish a sustainable financial industry. After the 1929 crash, in the midst of the Great Depression, Wall Street was able to reestablish public trust by building a financial industry based on a deep ethical commitment to clients that exceeded the minimum requirements of law. These values sustained the financial industry for over a half-century. In the years leading up to the financial crisis, Wall Street pursued a vastly different financial model, where profits were based on proprietary trading rather than serving clients. It became unmoored from the values that had sustained it for so long and sank to ethical standards that scraped along or broke below the legal minimum. Looking forward to the future, the challenge for Wall Street will be to develop a new set of values that will once again restore public trust and create the basis for a sustainable financial industry in the twenty-first century. Before we offer our thoughts on how Wall Street might lead its own moral instauration we will, in the next chapter, consider the role government can play in restoring public trust to the financial markets.

PART THREE

Policy Recommendations and Sustainable Values for Wall Street in the Twenty-First Century

Wall Street Regulation for the Twenty-First Century

Human greed isn't going to go away but you can put some limitations on it.

Paul Volcker

Introduction

Wall Street, enabled by accommodating government policies, has drifted far away from the business model that for a half-century efficiently allocated capital among American business ventures. Its profitability is no longer congruent with overall social welfare. This divergence between private profits and public welfare has become so great that Wall Street has fallen below even the minimal standard of corporate social responsibility advocated by free market icon Milton Friedman. The public can no longer rely on Wall Street to facilitate the flow of market information and help distribute capital to its most productive uses. Wall Street even deceived and lied to its own clients to generate profits and mitigate the losses it would suffer from trading misadventures in mortgage-backed securities. When the final reckoning came, it was taxpayers who had to pay the bill for Wall Street's self-inflicted wounds in the form of a massive government bailout.

This chapter describes the steps government has taken to restore integrity to financial markets, reduce systemic risk, and bring Wall Street back into alignment with Main Street. In particular, we focus on the Volcker Rule prohibitions on proprietary trading, as well as the regulation of derivatives and increased capital requirements limiting leverage.

Dodd-Frank

In economic terms, the financial crisis was a colossal "market failure," requiring, in the minds of a democratically controlled Congress, the heavy hand of government regulation. On July 21, 2010, President Barack Obama signed into law the Dodd-Frank Wall Street Reform and Consumer Protection Act ("Dodd-Frank" or the "Act") – the most comprehensive effort to overhaul financial industry regulation since the Great Depression. Dodd-Frank was enacted to contain systemic risks, avert another government bailout, and establish more comprehensive, coordinated, and vigilant regulatory oversight of capital markets. It provides a multifaceted, point-by-point and comprehensive response to the major factors contributing to the financial crisis (Table 6.1). Senator Christopher Dodd of Connecticut, co-sponsor of the Act, summarized its ambitious goals:

It will end bailouts, ensuring that failing firms can be shut down without relying on taxpayer bailouts or threatening the stability of our economy. It will create an advance warning system in the economy, so that there is always someone responsible looking out for the next big problem. It will ensure that all financial practices are exposed to the sunlight of transparency, so that exotic instruments like hedge funds and derivatives don't lurk in the shadows and businesses can compete on a level playing field.[1]

The Act was passed despite fierce opposition from Republican legislators. Typical was the view of Senator Richard Shelby of Alabama – ranking Republican member of the Banking, Housing, and Urban Affairs Committee – who described the bill in a broadside attack as "a legislative monster that expands the scope and power of ineffective bureaucracies, creates vast new bureaucracies with little accountability, and seriously undermines

Table 6.1. *Dodd-Frank: point-by-point response to causes of the financial crisis*

Problem	Solution
Systemic risk increased by the repeal of Glass-Steagall's separation of commercial and investment banks.	The Volcker Rule prohibits banks from engaging in proprietary trading. *(Section 619 – Prohibitions on proprietary trading and certain relationships with hedge funds and private equity funds)*
Excessive leverage creates overall systemic risk.	Require banks to undergo stress tests. See also Basel III. *(Section 165 – Enhanced supervision and prudential standards for nonbank financial companies supervised by the Board of Governors and certain bank holding companies)*
Hidden systemic risks of derivatives.	Empower the SEC and CFTC to regulate derivatives. *(Title VII – Wall Street Transparency and Accountability)*
Lack of overall coordinated regulation.	Creation of Financial Stability Oversight Council. *(Title I – Financial Stability)*
Failure of systemically important financial institutions could require government bailout.	Bans use of taxpayer funds to prevent liquidation of large financial companies. *(Title II – Orderly Liquidation Authority)*

Wall Street Regulation for the 21st Century

Problem	Solution
Lack of formal plans to deal with possible failure of a major financial institution.	Systemically vital financial institutions must provide a "living will" to facilitate "rapid and orderly resolution, in the event of material financial distress or failure." *(Section 165 – see above)*
Compensation systems create perverse incentives for excessive risk taking.	Require greater disclosure and shareholder input on executive compensation. *(Section 951 – Shareholder vote on executive compensation disclosures)*
Banks taking advantage of unwary consumers.	Establishment of the Consumer Financial Protection Bureau. *(Title X – Bureau of Consumer Financial Protection)*
Nonbank institutions like Lehman Brothers and hedge funds present huge systemic risk to the financial markets.	Increase supervision of large and systemically important hedge funds and other nonbank financial institutions. *(Title I – Financial Stability)*
Banks originating asset-backed securities offerings defraud customers.	Reforms asset-backed securitization process. *(Title IX. Subtitle D – Improvements to the Asset-Backed Securitization Process)*

the competitiveness of the American economy ... unfortunately, the bill does very little to make our system safer."[2] Mindful of such criticism, when the bill was passed President Obama declared, "the financial industry is central to our nation's ability to grow, to prosper, to compete and to innovate. This reform will foster that innovation, not hamper it."[3]

Two years after passage, Dodd-Frank's implementation remained mired in controversy, and a cloud of uncertainty hung over the financial industry. Even by Washington standards the process promised to be lengthy, complex, and contentious. Wall Street has mounted a substantial effort to at least influence and perhaps to delay and undermine implementation by regulators. Goldman Sachs alone has set up a twelve-person government affairs office in Washington.[4] Even after the financial crisis, after the TARP bailout, after the mass demonstrations and public discontent spurred by the Occupy Wall Street movement, and after collectively paying billions in fines and civil lawsuits, Wall Street executives remain fundamentally unrepentant and defiant. They also take perverse comfort in the complexity of the Act, entertaining the vain hope that the complexity itself somehow justifies inaction. A prime example is JPMorgan Chase CEO Jamie Dimon, the often-intemperate unofficial leader of the financial industry's fight to defend its interests. In March 2010, Dimon urged lawmakers to vote against the Act, claiming, "the new law ha[s] failed to improve the regulatory architecture ... we had a system of too many regulators, too much overlap and too many gaps. Instead of simplifying and strengthening, we added more. It's even more complicated now."[5] It seems an odd specter for an industry that thrives on complexity and technical wizardry to plead for simplicity when it comes to the method of their regulation. Indeed, much of the complexity arises from an attempt to accommodate the interests of industry. In 2012, two years after Dodd-Frank became law, Dimon continued to rail on against it, declaring, in a letter to shareholders, "financial reform has not been intelligent design." Nonetheless, he wryly pledged, JPMorgan Chase would adjust to the new regulatory environment, "whether or not we like it or think it is all needed."[6]

Federal regulatory agencies, slowly awakening from decades of slumber and cozy complicity with industry, have been uncertain and cautious in taking the reins of their new powers. A new era of Wall Street regulation has begun and it will require dedicated public servants to sharpen their tools and a new generation of regulators to develop new skill sets. They will have to compile, interpret, and act upon vast amounts of previously unreported data about matters never before subject to regulation. The law firm of Davis Polk and Wardwell LLP estimated that 200 rule-making actions and over 65 studies require completion before final implementation.[7] The former head of the Securities Industry Financial Management Association (SIFMA) predicted full implementation might take through 2016.[8] Moreover, regulators are understandably wary of the damage they might cause to an already fragile economy if they were to rush through basic reforms that are certain to shatter existing Wall Street business models and thereby disquiet jittery credit and financial markets. Financial lobbyists have attempted to prey on this fear by suggesting that stringent government regulations will hamper the competitiveness of American-based banks. However, to achieve sustainable profits, the global financial industry needs the United States' legal and regulatory system to lead and work in cooperation with other nations, not to engage in a self-defeating competitive race to the bottom. As we have seen in previous chapters, strong and effective government oversight helped assure the integrity and prosperity of American financial institutions for over a half-century after the 1929 stock market crash. One clear lesson of the financial crisis that should not be forgotten is that gratuitous deregulation can be as corrosive to Wall Street profitability as burdensome overregulation.

The Volcker Rule

Of the 2,300 pages in Dodd-Frank, the provision generating the most heated debate has been Section 619, the so-called Volcker Rule. This provision, suggested by and informally named after former Federal Reserve Board Chair Paul Volcker, prohibits proprietary trading by "insured depository institutions," including their affiliates. It prohibits such banks from engaging in proprietary trading of debt and equity securities, commodities, derivatives, or other financial instruments. "Proprietary trading" is very broadly defined as "acting as a principal for the trading account of a banking organization or supervised nonbank financial company in any transaction to purchase or sell, or otherwise acquire or dispose of: any security; any derivative; contract of sale of a commodity for future delivery; any option on any such security, derivative, or contract; or any other security or financial instrument that the appropriate federal banking agencies, the SEC, and the CFTC (the Regulators) may determine by rule."[9] In addition to prohibiting principal trading by banks themselves, the Volcker Rule also prohibits banking entities from "sponsoring" or "investing" in hedge funds or private equity funds. Significantly, it does not bar banks from lending to such funds.

Nobel Prize-winning economist Joseph Stiglitz and Robert Johnson, executive director of the Roosevelt Institute, described the rule's purpose in a letter submitted to the SEC:

> The Volcker Rule was drafted with an eye towards – and must be considered from – a systemic viewpoint. At its most basic, it forces a strong separation between hedge fund-like activities that deploy high risk in search of high reward, and depository lending banks, which should take modest risks to extend credit to families, small business, and the real economy generally.[10]

It should be noted that to accept TARP bailout funds, Morgan Stanley and Goldman Sachs each changed their legal status to become a bank holding company. As a result, both firms are now subject to the Dodd-Frank proscriptions on proprietary trading. The investment banking operations of JPMorgan Chase, Bank of America, and Citicorp, by virtue of their affiliations with federally insured banks, are also covered by the Act. In explaining the logic of the rule, Volcker himself emphasizes that banks have the protection of government guarantees such as through the Federal Deposit Insurance Corporation, and that if companies like Goldman Sachs and Morgan Stanley want to do speculative trading, they should "turn in their bank licenses."[11]

Dodd-Frank also substantially increased regulatory oversight and supervision of hedge funds and other non-banks where, given the restrictions of the Volcker Rule on banks, investment capital seeking profits from proprietary trading will inevitably migrate. In April 2012, the Financial Stability Oversight Council, headed by Treasury Secretary Timothy Geithner, adopted rules that enable certain nonbanks to be designated as "systemically important financial institutions." Among the requirements for this new category of nonbanks will be expanded registration information for their managers and a substantial increase in record keeping and reporting obligations. The initial triggers for such designation were a minimum of $50 billion in assets, $3.5 billion in derivative liability, and $20 billion in debt, with high leverage ratios also a potential triggering factor. Under these rules AIG and Lehman Brothers, two of the failed titans that brought down financial markets in 2008, would have qualified for this increased level of scrutiny. In the future, hedge fund firms such as Paulson & Co., investment managers such as BlackRock, investment companies such as Berkshire Hathaway, and the financing arms of large corporations such as GE Capital could all potentially be designated as systemically important financial institutions and subjected to higher levels of reporting and oversight.[12]

The Volcker Rule well illustrates the implementation challenges of Dodd-Frank. Government regulators seemed to deliberately invite wide-ranging scrutiny and skepticism when on October 11, 2011 they released a proposed draft of the regulations for public comment. The document was almost 300 pages long and posed nearly 1,000 questions on 400 topics.[13] By February 13, 2012, over 17,000 comment letters were received, of which less than 4 percent – approximately 650 letters – were in support of the proposed regulations.[14] Longtime financial industry observer James B. Stewart writing for *The New York Times* observed, "Wall Street firms have spent countless millions of dollars trying to water down the original Volcker proposal and have succeeded in inserting numerous exemptions."[15]

The financial industry's concerns about the Volcker Rule chiefly involve the distinction it makes between *market-making*, which banks are permitted to do, and *proprietary trading*, which they may not. Typical is the commentary by the Asset Management Group of SIFMA: "As asset managers, we believe that the proprietary trading provisions of the Proposal, if implemented, would drastically disrupt the liquidity that banking entities provide to our clients."[16] The concern is that financial institutions cannot effectively maintain a market for their clients without holding a significant inventory of securities for extended periods of time, and that this necessary component of market-making might run the risk of being considered a proprietary trade under the proposed SEC rules.

Paul Volcker himself believes it will be easy to distinguish between ordinary and speculative trading. "Do your market-making but don't mix up your proprietary trading with market-making," he admonishes.[17] However, JPMorgan Chase's Jamie Dimon does not believe it will be so easy to make the distinction. In characteristically colorful language, he recounts the difficulties traders will face when making decisions about what inventory they need to maintain to provide high-quality services to clients:

There are two parts. The part where they said no proprietary trading, we're fine with. We've never had an issue with that. The part about market-making is the part that everyone is writing ... about. We are a store. When you come to JP Morgan we give you great prices on corporate bonds, FX, interest rate trades. Most of the business is driven by clients and we have the widest and deepest capital markets in the world. Remember when a client calls up JP Morgan if we don't give them the best price we don't get the business. The best price is a huge benefit for them. That's not an insult. We don't make huge bets. So I understand the role is to make sure that companies don't make huge bets on the balance sheets, but market-making is just like these stores down the street when they buy a lot of polka dot dresses they hope they are going to sell. They're making a judgment call. They may be wrong. So protecting the system I agree with, but, talking about the intent, I tell you every trader will have to have a lawyer, compliance officer, doctor (to see what their testosterone levels are), and shrink – what's your intent. No we're going to make markets for our clients to give them the best products, the best services, the best research, and the best prices. That is a good thing, in spite of what Paul Volcker says.[18]

Others on Wall Street share Dimon's concerns. One longtime Wall Street trader who preferred to remain anonymous explained:

My loyalty now, frankly always, has been to my customers and my clients, they are the ones I really work for. Even though I am employed by "X" bank my customers are the ones that pay me and my job is to find them product they want at the best price. If we carry less inventory then it is going to be much harder for me to help my customers, and maybe then I will have to find the product in the market and that is going to be more expensive. I hope that does not happen, it won't be good for my customers or my business.[19]

There is, to be sure, a draconian aspect to the Volcker rule. Until the 1980s when proprietary trading started becoming a larger component of profits, Wall Street firms actively traded some fixed income and equity securities for their own accounts. It was natural, for example, for Salomon Brothers to take the knowledge it derived from market-making and to use it to generate some profits for the firm. The ethical problems came when the tail began to wag the dog and proprietary trading began to overshadow customer services. At that point proprietary trading began to pose risks for the integrity of client services, not to mention for the larger economy. Wall Street has only itself to blame for the broad ban of all proprietary trading. In fact, it should count itself lucky that Congress allowed the market-making exception at all because the question must be asked as to whether there is any reason at all that market-making activities must be conducted in financial institutions that also happen to be federally insured.

Experience will inform the determination of when inventory is being accumulated for proprietary trading and when it is being done to service customers. A related challenge will arise when attempting to draw the line between transactions that are entered into in order to prudently manage assets and decrease a bank's risk – a permitted activity under the Volcker Rule – and prohibited transactions that are intended as directional bets seeking greater firm profitability. In May 2012, JPMorgan Chase provided a dramatic example of the difficulty and potential import of this distinction when its Chief Investment Office reported a nearly $6 billion loss in hedging transactions purportedly designed to mitigate risk.[20] Notwithstanding the difficulty of drawing these lines in the right places, complexity is no excuse for inaction or regulatory sclerosis. Experience and accumulated knowledge will enable regulators to strike an appropriate balance between prudent bank practices and speculative transactions. Over time, rules will be adopted and then adapted, as necessary, to balance business realities with the aims of the Volcker Rule.

Re-regulation of Derivatives Transactions

As we have described previously, during the last year of the Clinton Administration former CFTC Commissioner Brooksley Born voiced strong opposition to passage of the Commodity Futures Trading Modernization Act of 2000, only to be shouted down by Treasury Secretary Robert Rubin, Federal Reserve Board chair Alan Greenspan, and SEC chair Arthur Levitt. The CFMA stripped Born's agency of statutory authority over the derivatives market. Some regard this as the most important regulatory development leading to the financial crisis.[21] The derivatives market eventually ballooned to $600 trillion, and it was only after the mortgage market collapsed that government regulators understood the true magnitude of the hidden systemic risk created by derivatives.

Title VII of Dodd-Frank repeals virtually all the exemptions related to over-the-counter (OTC) derivatives created by the CFMA.[22] The new statute was designed to increase transparency, reduce systemic risk, and promote market integrity within the financial system by, among other things, "(1) providing for the registration and comprehensive regulation of swap dealers and large end users ... ('major swap participants'), (2) imposing clearing and trade execution requirements on standardized OTC derivative products; (3) creating recordkeeping and real-time reporting regimes; and (4) imposing margin, capital, and position limits requirements on market participants."[23] Virtually every participant in the derivatives markets will be impacted.

One interesting aspect of Title VII is the division of authority between the CFTC and the SEC. The CFTC's regulatory authority includes "swaps, swap dealers and major swap participants, swap data repositories, derivative clearing organizations with regard to swaps, persons associated with a swap dealer or major swap participant, eligible contract participants, and swap execution facilities."[24] The SEC's powers, by contrast, relate to securities-based swaps; a new category created by Title VII that includes credit default swaps – a financial instrument at the heart of the 2008 crisis. By April 2012, the CFTC and the SEC had worked together to produce over seventy proposed and final rules. However, the complexity of these products and markets, including the difficulty of precisely defining securities-based swaps, means that there is likely to be an extended period of time before the SEC will be able to finalize the regulatory regime in this area.

Establishing market discipline, oversight, and transparency over derivatives, including swap transactions and credit derivative swaps, is quite obviously a critical response to the financial crisis. The increased transparency provides regulators with an early warning system of when risk in the financial system is elevated and where it might be located. It is less likely that firms like AIG and Bear Sterns would be able to accumulate such large derivative positions without government detection. Title VII also provides regulators with tools to control the risk once it has been identified.

Decreasing Leverage and Increasing Capital Requirements

After the collapse of Lehman Brothers in September 2008, the impact of the financial crisis quickly spread to every corner of the globe. In Iceland, the three largest banks were taken over by the government, and eventually the country had to be bailed out by the International Monetary Fund (IMF). This was the first time in over thirty years that a developed country received an IMF loan.[25] In Europe, credit markets froze, and vulnerable, highly leveraged borrowers faltered. Within two weeks of the bankruptcy of Lehman, it was reported that "governments from London to Berlin have seized or bailed out five faltering banks. In Ireland, where rumors of panicked withdrawals from banks spooked the stock market, the government offered a two-year blanket guarantee on all deposits and bank debt."[26] In the United Kingdom alone five banks were either nationalized or partially nationalized.[27] Of the 87 banks that availed themselves of the $700 billion TARP bailout, 43 were foreign, many of them European.[28]

Although Dodd-Frank is the most comprehensive effort to rein in the excesses of Wall Street, one of the most important post-financial crisis initiatives has originated from the Basel Committee on Banking Supervision, which is part of the Bank for International Settlements (BIS). This Swiss-based committee, with membership from every advanced economy, including the United States, has developed increasingly into a *de facto* standard-setting body on all aspects of global banking supervision.[29] The post-crisis Basel III proposal focuses squarely on bank capital requirements and aims to limit excessive leverage throughout the banking sector.[30] Basel III establishes new key capital ratio requirements that are more than double the previous levels and are scheduled to almost double again by 2019.[31]

Even though these efforts are aimed at shoring up the global banking system, some critics believe they are not tough enough. They argue that almost every bank will easily meet these supposedly stringent require- ments and that Basel III will not help prevent another credit crunch.[32] As is the case with the Volcker Rule in the United States, however, bank lobbyists are working overtime in Europe to water down and create loopholes in implementing legislation.[33] JPMorgan Chase CEO Jamie Dimon once again is leading the charge, arguing that "Basel III makes it worse" by requiring more capital to be held in risky assets at moments when more leverage is needed and warranted.[34] Despite such bluster by some banking industry officials, Christine Lagarde, managing director of IMF, believes that the work of fortifying and restoring the financial system and financial institutions in Europe is far from complete. At the August 2011 U.S. Federal Reserve Bank annual meeting of central bank- ers, Ms. Lagarde warned that European banks "must be strong enough to withstand the risks of sovereigns and weak growth. This is the key to cutting the chains of con- tagion. If it is not addressed, we could easily see the fur- ther spread of economic weakness to core countries, or even a debilitating liquidity crisis." She went on to sug- gest that forced capital injections into banks, possibly even with public funds, might be necessary.[35]

In the United States, efforts to verify the adequacy of bank capital have been undertaken by the Federal Reserve Bank through the administration of "stress tests" of bank balance sheets to gauge the capital adequacy of these banks under severely adverse macroeconomic scenarios specified by the Federal Reserve.[36] These stress tests, more formally referred to as the Comprehensive Capital Analysis and Review (CCAR), provide the Federal Reserve with vital information regarding the capital planning processes and capital adequacy of the largest banks in the country. In March 2012, the Federal Reserve released the results of the stress tests, reporting that of the 19 financial firms subject to the stress test, 18 had enough capital to continue operations in a steep economic downturn, defined in part to include sharp declines in housing prices and stock markets and unemployment at 13 percent.[37]

A related effort to control systemic risk has been the effort to assure that a bank will be able to fail without taking down other sectors of the financial markets – in essence, removing the possibility of being too big to fail. U.S. regulators have approved guidelines requiring the largest and most complex financial institutions, including Citigroup and JPMorgan Chase, to develop "living wills" with projected plans for how they would liquidate with minimal effect on other large actors and financial sectors.[38] Such living wills are part of a coordinated global agreement reached by the leaders of the Group of 20 nations in November 2011. The 29 most significant banks worldwide were required to submit draft recovery and resolution plans by June 2012.[39]

Conclusion

The net effect of the regulatory reforms enacted after the financial crisis will be more transparent, more accountable, and less highly leveraged financial institutions playing more specialized roles in facilitating capital markets. *Forbes* writer Hala Turyalai described post-Volcker Rule Wall Street with acidic precision: "While the Volcker Rule will surely put a damper on bank trading profits, it will force many firms to go back to the basic blocking and tackling of the financial services business – acting as intermediaries for their clients. It may also help the Fed, shareholders and taxpayers sleep better at night."[40]

Although we agree that effective regulation is an indispensable part of the solution, we also believe that efficient financial markets require a strong set of ethical beliefs and practices. This will especially be true as financial institutions adapt to the changes in the regulatory environment. There will be new business challenges, constraints, and relationships with clients, all of which will require substantial ethical reflection. Regrettably, the combination of regulatory caution and Wall Street's high stakes lobbying effort has resulted in legislative and moral gridlock. It will take years before the key provisions of the act are implemented; years until a new financial industry configuration emerges; years until it becomes clear what kinds of firms will prosper in the new business environment; and, most crucially, years until new executive leadership and corporate governance practices emerge to develop and nourish the values necessary to sustain a prosperous and socially responsible financial industry in the twenty-first century. Despite resistance from Wall Street, however, regulatory change is coming, and so too eventually will come an evolution of business values. In the final chapter, we look to the future and reflect upon the kinds of core values that will be required to restore public trust and support sustainable prosperity for Wall Street in the twenty-first century.

— ❖ CHAPTER SEVEN ❖ —

Wall Street Values for the Twenty-First Century

Introduction

Government can help align Wall Street interests with those of Main Street by channeling self-interested behavior into socially useful outcomes. It can serve as a watchdog, attempting to detect and prevent illegal behavior. Government cannot, however, replace the role of business ethics. Despite numerous regulatory failures and outsized errors in business judgment, the financial crisis was fundamentally a moral crisis. At great cost, we learned that greed, unless tempered by good values, does not "work" from a social perspective. Ethically unmoored, Wall Street became a danger to free markets, the economy, and itself. Only a massive public bailout saved it from the consequences of its own moral decay.

Wall Street today remains morally adrift. It no longer adheres to the customer-driven values that sustained it since the 1930s, yet it has not adopted values and ethical principles suitable for its evolving business models. It lurches along in a moral wasteland from which it may take years, if not decades, to emerge. The prototypical postmillennial Wall Street executive is ethically untroubled, even when securities sold to clients are virtually assured to lose value. Goldman Sachs CEO Lloyd Blankfein captured the essence of this moral sensibility when he described his formative experience at the firm's commodities trading unit: "We didn't have the word 'client' or 'customer,' we had "counterparties" – and that's because we didn't know how to spell the word 'adversary.'"[1] In an earlier era, Wall Street professionals would not have tolerated this kind of sentiment or rampant abuse of customers. However, the postmillennial financial executive lacks relevant principles for sound ethical judgment. The values of the past no longer apply, but no principles have emerged to replace them. In earlier chapters we analyzed how Wall Street arrived at this moral quagmire. In this chapter we consider the prospects for restoring values to a central role on Wall Street.

Moral "Moral Hazard"

No major financial industry leader has publicly acknowledged the role of ethics and values in the financial crisis.
(One exception is Robert G. Taft, the former chairman
of the Securities Industry and Financial Management
Association, who has called for an ethics of "Stewardship"
and service to others.)[2] The defining moment of this
moral obtuseness came during Mr. Blankfein's Senate
testimony. Senator Carl Levin pointedly asked him if
he felt remorse for how Goldman Sachs deceived and
abused its own clients. Blankfein replied that yes, he
was sorry for the plight of others. However, he felt com-
pelled to add, "I haven't heard anything today that
makes me think we did something wrong."[3] The consti-
tutional inability to acknowledge ethical shortcomings
is common on Wall Street. Typical is the assessment of
one Wall Street professional who bluntly rejected the
idea that values played any role in the financial crisis:
"the problem was not a change in ethics, but a failure
to understand the risk on and off the balance sheet.
Frankly no one understood the risks, not that we did
not want to or did not try to."[4]

Another illustration of Wall Street's unwillingness to
grapple with difficult ethical discussions was the reaction to the very public resignation of Greg Smith, head

of Goldman Sachs's U.S. equity derivatives business in Europe, the Middle East, and Africa. Writing in the Op-Ed pages of the *New York Times*, Smith sent shockwaves throughout the global financial community by charging that even after the firm issued a showy report purporting to reaffirm its values, "the interests of the client continue to be sidelined in the way the firm operates and thinks about making money." He went on to say, "decline in the firm's moral fiber represents the single most serious threat to its long-run survival…. It astounds me how little senior management gets a basic truth: If clients don't trust you they will eventually stop doing business with you. It doesn't matter how smart you are." Smith offered lurid details of "how callously people talk about ripping their clients off. Over the last 12 months I have seen five different managing directors refer to their own clients as 'muppets', sometimes over internal email."[5]

At Goldman Sachs the official reaction was complete denial. Top executives Lloyd Blankfein and Gary Cohn wrote to employees:

We were disappointed to read the assertions made by this individual that do not reflect our values, our culture and how the vast majority of people at Goldman Sachs think about the firm and the work it does on behalf of our clients. Everyone is entitled to his or her opinion. But it is unfortunate that an individual opinion about Goldman

Sachs is amplified in a newspaper and speaks louder than the regular, detailed and intensive feedback you have provided the firm and independent, public surveys of workplace environments.[6]

The rest of Wall Street closed ranks in sympathy with Goldman Sachs. JPMorgan Chase CEO Jamie Dimon cautioned his employees not to "seek advantage" of Goldman Sachs "alleged issues or hearsay," as though it was the unfortunate victim of baseless defamation. Morgan Stanley CEO James P. Gorman criticized the *New York Times* for running the piece and advised staffers not to circulate it.[7] Some dismissed Smith as an inconsequential, failed banker seeking vengeance because his compensation was "only" $500,000 a year. Not one leading Wall Street figure stepped up to say that Smith's resignation raised important issues meriting discussion and consideration.

A number of factors help explain the cosseted mentality of Wall Street executives on questions of ethics. The lack of vigor in government prosecutions is an important one. Within three months of the commencement of the SEC fraud charges in the Abacus case, for example, Goldman Sachs settled with the government. The $550 million fine was the largest ever paid for securities fraud. It was, however, essentially hush money, and the magnitude of the fine did not help establish any principles of responsibility.[8] According to the SEC, Goldman Sachs "agreed to settle the SEC's charges *without admitting or denying the allegations*"[9] (emphasis added).

In November 2011, U.S. District Court Judge Jed Rakoff expressed concern over the SEC's pattern of settling cases for large fines without any admission of guilt by the accused and delayed approval of Citicorp's $285 million settlement. Judge Rakoff questioned whether it was in the public interest to approve a settlement without an admission of guilt by Citicorp or some kind of acknowledgment that a legal line had been crossed. During the hearing, the judge asked a simple and penetrating question: "Why should the court impose a judgment in a case in which the SEC alleges a serious securities fraud, but the defendant neither admits nor denies wrongdoing?"[10] A big reason behind the continuing mentality of denial on questions of ethics is thus quite simply that Wall Street has been able to buy off any finding of culpability.

Another missed opportunity has been the failure of prosecutors to seek corporate integrity agreements as part of these settlements. Such agreements are common, for example, in the healthcare sector where they are administered by the Inspector General's Office of the Department of Health & Human Services and usually require compliance reforms, the development of standards and practices, and employee training. They sometimes involve appointing an outside monitor to oversee management's actions.[11] In the case of Wall Street, however, the government has relied on checkbook justice. Financial firms write a big check and, in return, they are able to pretend they did nothing wrong. The end result has been what we term "moral moral hazard."

The term "moral hazard" is a technical economic term that has often been used in connection with the government bailout. It describes the "perverse incentive" of someone who has insurance to engage in precisely the type of risky behavior he or she is insured against. The bailout created moral hazard in the sense that it confirmed the expectation of many Wall Street firms that, because they were "too big to fail," they could take on excessive risk and later rely on a government bailout if the risk did not work out. This economic moral hazard had been building for decades in the financial industry. In 1984, federal regulators offered a $4.5 billion rescue package for Continental Illinois bank. In 1998 the Federal Reserve Bank of New York organized a $3.625 billion bailout by other financial institutions of the Long-Term Capital Management hedge fund. Each bailout, whether using public or private funds, increased systemic moral hazard, culminating in the $700 billion TARP bailout during the 2008 financial crisis. It should be noted that Dodd-Frank explicitly rejects this kind of role for government. Or at least it takes it out of the hands of regulators.

Should the government be faced with another too-big-to-fail situation, Congress theoretically could pass another law reversing its position.

We want to suggest another kind of moral hazard occurring in the aftermath of the crisis. We call it *moral moral hazard*. (The repetition of the word "moral" is deliberate.) We intend this as an ethical, not economic, term. Moral moral hazard refers to the manner in which the settlement of all of the subsequent government court cases for cash without principled accountability has created perverse incentives for Wall Street to continue ignoring its moral failings and ethical challenges. Even after the home mortgage debacle, the financial crisis, and a global recession, after the TARP bailout, after Occupy Wall Street tapped into widespread public discontent with the industry, and after collectively paying billions in fines and civil lawsuits, Wall Street remains unrepentant. It clings to the fiction that its corrupt values and behaviors are part and parcel of a healthy free market system, when, in fact, these values continue to pose a threat to financial stability and the economy as a whole, and, as Greg Smith pointed out when resigning from Goldman Sachs, they constitute the "single, most serious threat"[12] to their own economic survival.

Notwithstanding the reluctance of Wall Street firms to give serious consideration to values, there are plenty of opportunities for proactive thinking about business ethics – before the next scandal, before the next major government fine, before government prosecutors subject the management of a major firm to a wide-ranging corporate integrity agreement or appoint an outside monitor to assure compliance with the law. Just as the 1933 and 1934 securities laws represented an economic opportunity for firms like Merrill Lynch to establish a business model based upon trust and client service, so today Dodd-Frank's regulatory reforms present a golden opportunity for a moral rebirth, a chance to develop appropriate values to complement evolving business models, preempt costly lawsuits and the loss of managerial discretion to an outside monitor, and earn back public trust. We want to highlight two areas where Wall Street can make significant ethical progress: conflicts of interest and compensation practices. Our discussion of these topics is not meant to be exhaustive, but to be suggestive of the ethical issues that will emerge in the 21st Century financial industry.

Conflicts of Interest

Wall Street broke down numerous regulatory barriers (and stretched others beyond recognition) in the three decades leading up to the financial crisis, but it did not give much thought to the ethical concerns likely to arise as a result. The combination of commercial banking with investment banking, securities origination with investment advising, and proprietary trading with customer service created significant conflicts of interest that have yet to be sufficiently appreciated on Wall Street. Without the integration of robust ethical principles into their corporate governance, human resource policies and operations, financial firms failed to detect these ethical conflicts. Until the 1980s when proprietary trading started becoming a larger component of profits, Wall Street firms actively traded fixed income and equity securities for their own accounts. It was natural, as we have noted, for Salomon Brothers to take the knowledge it derived from market making in bonds and to use it to generate some profits for the firm. The ethical problems came when proprietary trading began to overshadow customer services. At that point proprietary trading began to pose risks for the integrity of client services.

This "conflict creep" occurred at Goldman Sachs when its CDO origination business was located in the same business unit that was responsible for trading CDOs with the firm's own capital accounts. The traders in this business unit had neither the expertise nor the professional orientation to conduct the due diligence activities the firm would normally undertake before selling securities to its customers. After the financial crisis, the firm moved its CDO origination activities into the investment banking division. This was essentially an admission that the earlier organizational structure had created a structural conflict of interest between the firm and its clients.[13]

Our purpose in discussing this conflict of interest example from the past is to emphasize the lessons one can draw for the future. Regulatory authorities have reestablished some of the lines that had been previously blurred and have drawn a few that had not before existed. We want to suggest that it is critical for Wall Street firms to take a thoughtful ethical approach to working within those lines and that they be especially vigilant about client conflicts when, as is inevitable, they push the boundaries of the Volcker Rule and other post-crisis reforms. We have learned from nearly a century of securities regulation that, because of the vast sums of money at stake, creative and aggressive Wall Street professionals will always push the envelope on what is legally permissible as they innovate and develop new products and services for clients. They are likely in this regard to be a step ahead of the regulators. We are mindful that aggressiveness and innovation are hallmarks of a vigorous financial system. We believe, however, that a strong ethical compass can temper this drive and creativity so as to make Wall Street more responsible and ultimately more sustainable economically. The key is that when legal lines are being pushed and blurred, Wall Street needs to give thought to the underlying ethical concerns that may emerge.

One area where conflicts of interest are likely to arise is in the relationships between banks and nonbank financial institutions. There will be a great temptation for Wall Street firms to satisfy their appetite for risk by structuring complex and dynamic relationships with hedge funds. Although hedge funds will be more highly regulated after Dodd-Frank, their ability to deploy risk capital and generate superior returns will remain, relative to traditional investment banks, unencumbered. Wall Street firms that are themselves proscribed from proprietary trading by the Volcker Rule will try to remain relevant by marketing high value-added financial services and advice to these hedge funds. However, as profitable as these services will be, they will never provide the kinds of returns on capital that Wall Street has become accustomed to generating through proprietary trading. As a result, it seems inevitable that Wall Street will spend a substantial amount of time and money to determine legally innovative ways to develop new or revised business relationships and transactions with hedge funds that might enable Wall Street firms to maintain an economic interest in the kinds of risk-based capital businesses in which hedge funds specialize. Wall

Street's "prime brokerage" services have been highly profitable and hold the potential to be even more so. The leading providers of such prime brokerage services to hedge funds are JPMorgan Chase and Goldman Sachs, with Morgan Stanley a distant third.[14]

An indication as to how economically intertwined the relationships between banks and hedge funds have already become can be gleaned from JPMorgan Chase's marketing pitch for its prime brokerage services:

Whether clients' needs are in global execution, financing, clearing, portfolio management or asset servicing, we are committed to strategically partnering with our clients to help them build more effective and dynamic businesses.

Through their prime brokerage relationship, our clients have full access to the vast capabilities and global resources of the entire J.P. Morgan franchise, from the firm's preeminent investment bank and world-class strategic advisory services to the firm's insightful content and thought leadership of its research, conferences and client events.[15]

These kinds of "strategic" relationships between hedge funds and Wall Street firms create a wide array of risks for other customers and financial markets generally. Not all clients of Wall Street firms will be treated equally on postmillennial Wall Street. Large hedge funds will have preferred access to research and other bank services, and this raises complex ethical issues about conflicts of interest between the bank and its various clients that will need to be vetted and managed.

The preferential treatment of clients in sharing firm research has been a recurrent ethical issue for a number of Wall Street firms. In 2004 several firms collectively paid a $1.4 billion settlement to resolve accusations that they were issuing overly optimistic stock research to lure lucrative investment banking business. The settlement called for banks to put up a wall between research and investment banking. It was not long, however, before banks found another strategy to use their analytical capabilities to selectively benefit more important clients. In April 2012, Goldman Sachs agreed to pay $11 million each to the SEC and the Financial Industry Regulatory Authority to settle allegations that it did not have adequate policies in place to stop research tips from being selectively passed to only its preferred clients in the hopes of winning increased trading commissions. (Massachusetts regulators had settled a similar complaint with the firm in 2010.) According to the SEC, top clients received preferential treatment through the firm's trading "huddles", in which the bank's research analysts met with firm traders and select customers. SEC enforcement chief Robert S. Khuzami said the firm "failed to implement policies and procedures that adequately controlled the risk that research analysts could preview upcoming ratings changes with select traders and clients."[16]

A number of potential conflicts of interest issues are highlighted as a result of the regulatory attention on Goldman Sachs's huddle program. The involvement of the firm's trading desk in the evaluation of analysts had the potential to influence analysts to issue opinions that would promote trading and thus affect their objectivity. Favoring larger preferred clients by giving them selective access to research created a conflict of interest for the firm when it simultaneously conducted trades for smaller, non-preferred clients who might not have access to that research. What is most striking about the huddling incident is how clearly it demonstrates that after Senate hearings, after hundreds of millions of dollars spent on settling lawsuits related to client abuse, and after issuing a glossy report on its purportedly higher ethical standards, Goldman Sachs still does not have adequate corporate governance practices in place to identify and manage fundamental ethical issues involving how it treats clients. After all it has been through in recent years, this latest incident is another display of operational ineptitude in ethics management from a firm that once prided itself on stellar management controls and teamwork.

Client conflicts have long presented ethical challenges for Wall Street. For example, in a merger or acquisition, the same firm might have acted as an advisor to both parties in the transaction. However, the conflicts of the twenty-first century will take on a more complex and opaque character. As the financial industry reconfigures itself in response to Dodd-Frank, banks will view some clients as strategic partners with the possibility of facilitating the bank's appetite for risking capital, and others as mere clients who receive more routine services. Such client conflicts will be a central ethical challenge in post-millennial Wall Street, and they will require study, vigilance and focused managerial execution.

Compensation Practices

In the wake of the financial crisis, considerable attention already has been devoted to the role of compensation. Dodd-Frank gave shareholders a "say on pay." As a result, every three years shareholders are entitled to cast a non-binding vote on executive compensation.[17] One noteworthy example of shareholders exercising such new power occurred in April 2012 when a majority of Citigroup's voting shareholders rejected a proposed executive compensation package.[18] Many firms have reformed their compensation plans in recognition of the "tail" risks associated with booked trading profits, adopting "claw backs" to take back bonuses if the executive's division posts a loss in a subsequent reporting period. In February 2012, for example, Swiss-based UBS bank (following a trading scandal that cost the bank $2.3 billion) took back 50 percent of bonuses awarded in 2011.[19] Although these developments introduce needed accountability, transparency, and shareholder input, many crucial ethical questions about compensation remain.

In the new regulatory environment, compensation design will have a significant impact on legal compliance and adherence to high ethical standards. One example concerns a class of proprietary trades permitted by the Volcker Rule. The *Wall Street Journal* reported in April 2012, that Bruno Iksil, a JPMorgan Chase trader known as the "London Whale" in the bank's United Kingdom-based Chief Investment Office – where trades are done to balance the assets and liabilities of the bank – took out an extremely large position in credit default swaps. Mr. Iksil was essentially betting that the creditworthiness of a group of companies would improve. The trade was done avowedly to hedge structural risks and investments and to bring the bank's asset and liabilities into better alignment.[20] The Volcker rule contains an exemption for such "asset-liability management," although it seems odd on the face of it that a bank, normally plenty exposed to borrower creditworthiness, would be by doubling down its bet on creditworthiness. Whatever the ultimate merits of

JPMorgan Chase's legal position on this issue, it would be interesting to know more about how the traders in the Chief Investment Office are compensated. If such putatively risk-reducing bets turn out to be highly profitable, will the traders be rewarded with some sort of bonus? Likely so. However, if the bonus for results is very large, it might be viewed by some as an indication that the traders are being rewarded for generating proprietary trading profits rather than for prudently managing assets and liabilities. Moreover, if the bank rewards the traders for their success in placing a bet, this could create incentives for traders to place larger proprietary bets in the future.

The distinction between asset-liability management and proprietary trading is a fine one, and substantial thought should, therefore, be given to how incentives created by compensation practices might encourage traders either to violate or stay within the bounds of legally permissible behavior. As it turns out, the "London Whale" trade turned out to be spectacularly wrong, losing nearly $6 billion and calling into question whether the trade was meant to hedge the bank's risk or as a thinly veiled form of proprietary trading. If compensation policies were properly structured, they would reward traders in the Chief Investment Office for neutralizing risk rather than for generating profits through trades that increase overall risk.

A similar issue arises in the grey area between market making and proprietary trading. The Volcker Rule prohibitions on proprietary trading are intended to return the focus of federally insured banks to executing trades for customers. Nevertheless, the rule expressly permits transactions in furtherance of making a market in securities intended for sales to customers. JPMorgan Chase CEO Jamie Dimon has expressed concerns that the Volcker Rule "constrains our ability to actively make markets or to competitively provide derivatives to our clients."[21] Here again, compensation practices have the potential to create incentives that encourage traders either to comply with the law or to step beyond its bounds. If banks take their avowed goal of satisfying customers seriously, then compensation for traders should reflect superior client service. Thus, a large component of a trader's compensation should be based on client satisfaction and customer revenues, rather than on profits the trader might have collaterally made for the firm through transactions required to make a market in a security. Obviously, the trader must also be evaluated by how efficiently he or she makes a market, but, to stay within the bounds of the law and to further better client service, compensation incentives should prioritize customer service and not profits from proprietary trading. It is a subtle distinction requiring carefully crafted compensation practices informed by legal and ethical principles.

Conclusion: Evolving Business Models, Evolving Values

Several years after the passage of Dodd-Frank, regulators charged with implementing the law still have much work to do. As a result, the future regulatory environment of the financial industry remains uncertain. Business models are in a period of rapid transformation, and it is unclear what kinds of financial institutions will emerge and how they will interact with each other, with other sectors of the economy, and with clients. Wall Street firms like Goldman Sachs, JPMorgan Chase, Deutsche Bank, Citicorp, Morgan Stanley and others clearly strain against the weight of the new regulations. They attempt to bend and shape the new rules so as to continue to pursue high risk, high reward strategies, while simultaneously conducting less lucrative but steady customer service-oriented businesses. The ethical issues we have discussed thus far – conflicts of interest and compensation incentives – derive from this fundamental tension between the old business model and the evolving regulatory environment. While the future economic survival of these types of complex, all-under-one-roof financial institutions is far from certain, the viability of all 21st century Wall Street firms will require adherence to a new set of values and ethical principles.

Competition is coming at traditional Wall Street institutions from seemingly every direction. On the trading side of the business, hedge funds, less encumbered by Dodd-Frank restrictions such as the Volcker Rule, are attracting ever more professional talent and investment capital. The migration of talent from traditional investment banks to hedge funds has been going on for two decades because of the potential for greater financial rewards. This trend is likely to accelerate because the kind of trading that will still be possible in traditional banks will be severely restricted and will not require, or indeed even allow, the full skill and creativity of the most aggressive traders. Capital investment is likely to follow the exodus of talent. Along with the talent and the capital, much of the systemic risk will also shift from traditional banks to the hedge funds, a development anticipated by Dodd-Frank, but that, nevertheless, will require increasing vigilance by regulators.

Competition is also developing on the customer side of the business where there are faint signs of rebirth for the client-focused model pioneered by Charles Merrill and others in the wake of the 1929 stock market crash. Wealth management firms are incorporating business models that attempt to more tightly align the interests of clients with those of their employees and shareholders. Many of these firms are being organized as investment advisors. (Whereas brokers are required only to provide advice "suitable" to customers at the moment of the sale, registered investment advisors [RIA] are required by the Investment Company Act of 1940 to put their clients' interests ahead of their own, and they are held to a fiduciary standard of responsibility to clients.) Here, too, there could be a significant exodus of talent and capital. Robert Mooney, a veteran of Merrill Lynch's global wealth management business and now CEO of the newly formed Snowden Capital Advisors, has said that he hopes to lure away advisers "who seek independence from any push to sell proprietary products, which is common at the brokerage arms of big banks."[22] A 2012 survey of financial advisors found that "younger advisors show even more proclivity for independence, with 65 percent of those surveyed who are under the age of 40 finding the idea of becoming an RIA appealing, compared to 43 percent of those age 40 and over."[23]

It should be noted that proposed regulatory changes also have the potential to redefine relationships with customers. Dodd-Frank directed the SEC to examine the benefits of new, uniform, fiduciary standards for broker-dealers. After completing a detailed study, the

SEC recommended "a uniform fiduciary standard of conduct for broker-dealers and investment advisers – no less stringent than currently applied to investment advisers under the Advisers Act – when those financial professionals provide personalized investment advice about securities to retail investors."[24] However, reflecting both the political and economic complexity of adopting and implementing such a standard, in January 2012, SEC chair Mary Shapiro announced the delay of the final regulations pending additional cost-benefit analysis.[25]

Competition is even coming at traditional Wall Street firms from their own clients. In April 2012, Blackrock Inc., a leading money manager and very large and important customer of Wall Street's trading desks, announced that it was planning to launch a "trading platform that would let the world's largest money manager and its peers bypass Wall Street and trade bonds directly with one another."[26] Even though this initiative is in the early stages and large money managers may decide not to share bid and offer prices with each other, the fact that institutional customers would even consider such an option speaks volumes about the general level of dissatisfaction with the market-making services they are receiving from the traditional investment banks.

While we have briefly surveyed some of the initial signals about the effects of Dodd-Frank on the Wall Street business model, just a few years removed from the financial crisis and in the middle of a sea change in regulatory reform it is difficult to predict what kinds of business models and which firms will dominate Wall Street in the twenty-first century. One thing is certain, however, based on the lessons of this book: values and business ethics will play an indispensable role in the growth and sustainable prosperity of the financial industry and the larger economy. We have attempted to demonstrate how flawed values and substandard business ethics brought ruin upon Wall Street and triggered a global recession causing immeasurable human suffering. Ordinary citizens are justifiably outraged about Wall Street's failures. We believe that unless Wall Street values and business ethics improve, the public will remain at risk.

In recent years, considerable attention has been devoted to the idea that "ethics pays." The proposition that good business ethics improves financial performance has become a mantra for those seeking to promote business ethics and has generated substantial academic research on the putative empirical relationship between ethics and profits.[27] We agree that, under certain circumstances, ethics and values can add to the bottom line and help assure the sustainability of a business enterprise. However, the financial crisis revealed that when the regulatory environment lacks intelligent design and vigilance what we have termed "profit disjunction" occurs. Undeniably Wall Street firms and their employees prospered greatly as they were setting the stage for the rest of society to suffer. The prosperity was temporary, to be sure, and poor business ethics ultimately undermined long-term profitability, but large fortunes were made over a very long period of time when Wall Street profits came at the expense of the economy as whole. Very little of those personal fortunes has been retrieved by shareholders or the public. There is simply no way to sugarcoat the fact that unethical behavior can sometimes pay very handsomely on Wall Street. Thus, one clear lesson of the financial crisis is the need for more effective laws and regulations to counteract temptation and greed.

We have attempted in this book to provide lawmakers and regulators with some tools for effective oversight. Law and regulation however, can accomplish only so much. History has shown that financial traders, executives, and other professionals will find and exploit gaps and loopholes in the legal system. Because no amount of regulation can control these impulses, effective management of organization ethics remains indispensable to a sustainable economy. The financial markets simply cannot work effectively and efficiently unless executives who manage financial institutions do so with appropriate values, good business ethics and adroit management skills. Although this book has been unsparing in its criticism, we hope it might inspire some Wall Street executives and boards of directors to lead a much needed managerial transformation and ethical rebirth. With power and good fortune comes great responsibility. It is critical that Wall Street professionals respect the crucial role they play in our collective prosperity. The financial system that feeds them is the same one that serves the entire economy, and to be sustainable, it must be nourished by appropriate values. There is much work to be done. We hope that this book can help start an urgently needed conversation on Wall Street about values and business ethics norms.

Notes

Chapter One   A Financial, Governmental, and Moral Crisis

1 Owens, L. A. (2011). "Confidence in banks, financial institutions and Wall Street." *Public Opinion Quarterly, 76*(1), 142–162. Available at http://ssrn.com/abstract=1931908. Retrieved on October 14, 2012.

2 Bradley, E. S., Teweles, R. J., & Teweles, T. M. (1992). *The stock market* (6 ed.). New York: Wiley.

3 111th Congress of the United States of America. (2010). *Dodd-Frank Wall Street Reform and Consumer Protection Act.*

4 Owens, L.A. (2011).

5 McLean, B., & Nocera, J. (2011). *All the devils are here: the hidden history of the financial crisis.* New York: Penguin Group.

6 Lewis, M. (2010). *The big short: inside the doomsday machine.* New York: W. W. Norton, p. 202.

Chapter Two Does Wall Street Have Any Responsibility to Society?

1 Paine, L. S. (2002). *Value shift: why companies must merge social and financial imperatives to achieve superior performance*. New York: McGraw Hill.

2 Donaldson, T., & Dunfee, T. (2002). *Ties that bind: a social contracts approach to business ethics*. Boston, MA: Harvard Business School Press.

3 Warren, E. (2011). *On debt crisis, fair taxation*, Web video. Available at http://www.youtube.com/watch?v=htX2usfqMEs. Retrieved on July 3, 2012.

4 Scherer, A. G., Palazzo, G., & Baumann, D. (2006). "Global rules and private actors: toward a new role of the transnational corporation in global governance." *Business Ethics Quarterly*, 16(4), 505–532.

5 Freeman, E. R., Harrison, J. S., & Wicks, A. C. (2007). *Managing for stakeholders: survival, reputation, and success*. New Haven, CT: Yale University Press.

6 *Guth v. Loft, Inc.*, 5 A2d 503 (Del. Ch. 1939).

7 *The Economist*. (2012, January 7). "B corps: Firms with benefits." Available at http://www.economist.com/node/21542432. Retrieved on July 5, 2012.

8 Friedman, M. (1970, September 13). "The social responsibility of business is to increase its profits." *New York Times Magazine*.

9 Werhane, P. H. (1991) *Adam Smith and his legacy for modern capitalism*. Oxford University Press.

10 Nicholson, W. & Snyder, C. (2008). *Microeconomic theory: basic principles and extension*. (10th ed.). Mason, OH: Thompson South-Western.

11 Nozick R. (1977). *Anarchy, state, and utopia*. New York: Basic Books.

12 Friedman, M. (1962). *Capitalism and freedom.* Chicago: University of Chicago Press.

13 Goldman Sachs. (2008). *2007 annual report.* Available at http://www.goldmansachs.com/investor-relations/financials/archived/annual-reports/attachments/entire-2007-annual-report.pdf. Retrieved on July 5, 2012.

14 Ball, D. (2012, February 9). "A first for UBS: bonus clawbacks." *Wall Street Journal*, p. C3.

15 McLean, B., & Nocera, J. (2011).

16 O'Leary, K. (2010, February 6). "The great recession: will construction workers survive?" *Time.* Available at http://www.time.com/time/nation/article/0,8599,1960639,00.html. Retrieved on July 5, 2012.

17 O'Leary, K. (2010).

Chapter Three   The Gathering Storm

1 Breyer, S. (1984). *Regulation and its reform.* Cambridge, MA: Harvard University Press.

2 The Financial Crisis Inquiry Commission. (2011). *The financial crisis inquiry report: final report of the national commission on the causes of the financial and economic crisis in the United States.* Washington: U.S. Printing Office, p. xvii.

3 GNMA Mortgage-Backed Securities Dealers Association. (1978). *The Ginnie Mae Manual.* Homewood, IL: Dow Jones-Irwin.

4 McLean, B., & Nocera, J. (2011), p. 13–14.

5 Ashcraft, A. B., & Schuermann, T. (2008). *Understanding the securitization of subprime mortgage credit, Staff Report No. 318.* New York: Federal Reserve Bank of New York.

6 Ashcraft & Schuermann. (2008).

7 Phillips, S. (2011, December 3). Private communication to authors.

8 The Financial Crisis Inquiry Commission. (2011).

9 *Investment Co. Inst. v. Camp*, 401 U.S. 617 (1971).

10 For two differing perspectives on the impact of a 2004 SEC ruling pertaining to net capital requirements see: Pickard, L. A. (2008, August 8). "SECs old capital approach was tried and true." *American Banker*, p. 10 and Cohen W., (2012, June) "How we got the crash wrong." *The Atlantic*.

11 Stiglitz, J. (2010). *Freefall: America, Free Markets, and the Sinking of the World Economy*. New York: W. W. Norton & Company. p. 163.

12 106th Congress of the United States of America. (2000). *Commodity Futures Modernization Act*.

13 Tett, G. (2009). *Fool's gold*. New York: Free Press.

14 Born, B. (1998, July 24). *Testimony before the U.S. House of Representatives Banking and Financial Services Committee*. Available at http://www.cftc.gov/opa/speeches/opaborn-33.htm. Retrieved on July 11, 2012.

15 Greenspan, A. (2003, July 16). *Hearing before the U.S. Senate Committee on Banking, Housing, and Urban Affairs*. Available at http://frwebgate.access.gpo.gov/cgi-bin/getdoc.cgi?dbname=108_senate_hearings&docid=f:91369.wais. Retrieved on March 11, 2012.

16 Tett, G. (2009).

17 The Financial Crisis Inquiry Commission. (2011), p.xxi.

18 Hirsch, M. (2010). *Capital offense: how Washington's wise men turned America's future over to wall street*. Hoboken, NJ: Wiley.

19 Hirsch, M. (2010).

20 Lewis, M. (2010); Zuckerman, G. (2010). *The greatest trade ever: the behind-the-scenes story of how John Paulson defied wall street and made financial history*. New York: Random House.

21 Paulson, H. M. Jr. (2010). *On the brink: inside the race to stop the collapse of the global financial system*. New York: Business Plus, pp. 337, 365.

Chapter Four   From Financial Services to Proprietary Trading

1 Wyckoff, P. (1972). *Wall street and the stock market*. Philadelphia, PA: Chilton Book Company.

2 Galbraith, J. K. (2009). *The great crash 1929*. New York: Houghton Mifflin Harcourt, pp. 60–63.

3 Galbraith. (2009).

4 Securities and Exchange Commission. (2009). *The investor's advocate: how the SEC protects investors, maintains market integrity, and facilitates capital formation*. Available at http://www.sec.gov/about/whatwedo.shtml. Retrieved on July 16, 2011.

5 Mayer, M. (1955). *Wall street: men and money*. New York: Harper & Brothers.

6 Perkins, E. J. (1999). *Wall Street to main street: Charles Merrill and middle-class investors*. Cambridge University Press, p. 253–254.

7 Merrill Lynch & Co. (1971). 1970 Annual report.

8 NYSE Euronext. "History." Available at http://www.nyse.com/about/history/1089312755484.html. Retrieved on July 17, 2011.

9 Morrison, A. D., & Wilhelm, W. J., Jr. (2007). *Investment banking: institutions, politics, law*. Oxford University Press.

10 Blankenberg, S., & Palma, J. G. (2009). "Introduction: the global financial crisis." *Cambridge Journal of Economics*, 33(4), 531–538.

11 Philippon, T., & Reshef, A. (2009). *Wages and human capital in the U.S. financial industry: 1909–2006*. Cambridge, MA: The National Bureau of Economic Research. Retrieved on July 16, 2012.

12 Paine, L. S., & Santoro, M. A. (1994). *Forging the new Salomon*. Boston, MA: Harvard Business School Publishing.

13 Holland, K., Himelstein, L., & Schiller, Z. (1995, October 10). "The Bankers Trust tapes." *Business Week*. Available at

http://www.businessweek.com/1995/42/b34461.htm.Retrieved on July 14, 2012.

14 Pollack, A., & Wayne, L. (1998, June 3). "Ending suit, Merrill Lynch to pay California county $400 million." *New York Times.* Available at http://www.nytimes.com/1998/06/03/business/ending-suit-merrill-lynch-to-pay-california-county-400-millio n.html?pagewanted=all&src=pm. Retrieved on July 13, 2012.

15 Dungey, D. (2007, April 28). *Calculated risk: finance and risk,* [Blog entry]. Available at http://www.calculatedriskblog.com/2007/04/ranieri-on-mbs-market-its-broke.html. Retrieved on March 17, 2012.

16 Lehman Brothers. (2007). 2007 *Annual report.* Available from http://lehman.rclclients.com/annual/2006/download/lbar_2006.pdf p. 84. Retrieved on July 18, 2011.

17 Ashcraft, A. B., & Schuermann, T. (2008).

Chapter Five   Secrets and Lies

1 Levin, Senator Carl. (2010). Opening Statement of Senator Carl Levin, U.S. Senate Permanent Subcommittee on Investigations Hearing, Wall Street and the Financial Crisis: The Role of Investment Banks. Available at http://www.levin.senate.gov/newsroom/press/release/?id=adbfc45a-1147–4a3f-9547–9f3c9efa4848. Retrieved on March 15, 2011.

2 Lewis, M. (2010); Zuckerman, G. (2010).

3 Permanent Subcommittee on Investigations, U.S. Senate. (2011). *Wall Street and the financial crisis: anatomy of a financial collapse.* Washington: U.S. Senate, p. 385.

4 Permanent Subcommittee on Investigations, U.S. Senate. (2011), p. 398.

5 For an account of Merrill Lynch's lax risk management practices, see McLean, B., & Nocera, J. (2011), especially chapter 8, "The Dumb Guys," pp. 308–321.

6 For a detailed account of how Goldman Sachs went from long to short positions on subprime mortgage investments, see Cohan, W. (2011). *Money and power: how Goldman Sachs came to rule the world*. New York: Doubleday, pp. 499–546.

7 Permanent Subcommittee on Investigations, U.S. Senate. (2011), p. 8.

8 Hayes, S. L., & Hubbard, P. M. (1990). *Investment banking: a tale of three cities*. Boston, MA: Harvard Business School Press.

9 Cassidy, J. (2002). *Dot.com: how America lost its mind and money in the internet era*. New York: Harper Collins.

10 McLean, B., & Nocera, J. (2011).

11 Permanent Subcommittee on Investigations, U.S. Senate. (2011), p. 379.

12 Goldman Sachs. (2008). 2007 *annual report*. Available at http://www.goldmansachs.com/investor-relations/financials/archived/annual-reports/attachments/entire-2007-annual-report.pdf. Retrieved on July 5, 2012.

13 Permanent Subcommittee on Investigations, U.S. Senate. (2011), p. 8.

14 Permanent Subcommittee on Investigations, U.S. Senate. (2011), p. 9.

15 Permanent Subcommittee on Investigations, U.S. Senate. (2011), p. 374.

16 Permanent Subcommittee on Investigations, U.S. Senate. (2011), p. 540.

17 Permanent Subcommittee on Investigations, U.S. Senate. (2011), p. 541.

18 Permanent Subcommittee on Investigations, U.S. Senate. (2011), p. 560.

19 Securities and Exchange Commission. (2010). *SEC charges Goldman Sachs with fraud in structuring and marketing of CDO tied to subprime mortgages* [press release]. Available at http://www.sec.gov/news/press/2010/2010-59.htm. Retrieved on June, 15, 2011.

20 Permanent Subcommittee on Investigations, U.S. Senate. (2011), p. 541.

21 Permanent Subcommittee on Investigations, U.S. Senate. (2011), p. 7.

22 Securities and Exchange Commission. (2011) SEC Enforcement Action. *J.P. Morgan to pay $153.6 million to settle SEC charges of misleading investors in CDO tied to U.S. housing market.* Available at http://www.sec.gov/spotlight/enf-actions-fc.shtml. Retrieved on October 22, 2011.

23 Securities and Exchange Commission. (2011). SEC Enforcement Action. *Citigroup to pay $285 million to settle SEC charges for misleading investors about CDO tied to housing market.* Available at http://www.sec.gov/spotlight/enf-actions-fc.shtml. Retrieved on October 22, 2011.

24 Fitzpatrick, D., & Eaglesham, J. (2011, April 4). "Wachovia targeted over sale of CDOs." *Wall Street Journal.* Available at http://online.wsj.com/article/SB10001424052748704587004576241102360892680.html. Retrieved on July 15, 2012,

25 Lehman Brothers. (2011, September 10). *Lehman announces preliminary third quarter results and strategic restructuring* [press release]. Available at http://www.ft.com/intl/cms/e0b164a0–7f32–11dd-a3da-000077b07658.pdf. Retrieved on September 10,2011.

26 United States Bankruptcy Court Southern District of New York. (2011, March 11). *In re Lehman Brothers Holdings Inc., et al., Debtors*

Report of Anton R. Valukas, Examiner. Chapter 11, Case No. 08–13555 (JMP).

27 de la Merced, M. J., & Sorkin, A. R. (2010, March 11). "Report details how Lehman hid its woes." *New York Times.* Available at http://www.nytimes.com/2010/03/12/business/12lehman.html. Retrieved on September 10, 2011.

28 *Dodona v. Goldman Sachs & Co.,* 7497 F. Supp. 2d (Southern District of New York 2012).

29 *Landesbanke Baden-Wurttemberg v. Goldman Sachs & Co.,* 7549 F. Supp. 2d (Southern District of New York 2011).

30 Permanent Subcommittee on Investigations, U.S. Senate. (2011), p. 502.

31 Permanent Subcommittee on Investigations, U.S. Senate. (2011), p. 503.

32 Goldman Sachs. (2006). Hudson High Grade Funding Offering Circular. Available from http://fcic-static.law.stanford.edu/cdn_media/fcic-docs/2006–10–00_Hudson%20High%20Grade%20Funding%202006–1_CDO%20Offering%20Circular.pdf. Retrieved on November 14, 2011.

33 *S.E.C. v. Goldman Sachs & Co.,* 790 F. Supp. 2d 147 (Southern District of New York 2011).

34 Goldman Sachs. (2006). Hudson High offering circular.

35 *Dodona v. Goldman Sachs & Co.,* 7497 F. Supp. 2d (Southern District of New York 2012).

36 *S.E.C. v. Citigroup,* 753 F. Supp. 2d 206, 235 (Southern District of New York 2010).

37 Goldman Sachs. (2011). *Report of the Business Standard Committee.* Available at http://www2.goldmansachs.com/who-we-are/business-standards/committee-report/business-standards-committee-report-pdf.pdf. Retrieved on August 20, 2011.

38 Goldman Sachs. (2011). *Report of the Business Standard Committee.*

Chapter Six Wall Street Regulation for the Twenty-First Century

1 Dodd, C. (2010, June). "Dodd statement on wall street reform." Speech presented at the U.S. Capitol, Washington, D.C. Available at http://banking.senate.gov/public/index.cfm?FuseAction=Newsroom.PressReleases&ContentRecord_id=2341c1eb-0afc-d694–5411–7c4ea6e96e21&Region_id=&Issue_id=. Retrieved on November 20, 2011.

2 Shelby, R. (2010, July). "Shelby: Dodd-frank act not real reform, just more of the same." Speech presented at the U.S. Capitol, Washington, D.C. Available at http://shelby.senate.gov/public/index.cfm/speeches?ID=72b086d5–6555–4f49-a315–4468da83e389. Retrieved on November 20, 2011.

3 Obama, B. (2010, July). "Remarks by the president on the passage of financial regulatory reform." Speech presented at the White House, Washington, D.C. Available at http://www.whitehouse.gov/the-press-office/remarks-president-passage-financial-regulatory-reform. Retrieved on April 7, 2012.

4 Tse, T. M. (2010, April 29). "Goldman Sachs adds to its ranks of lobbyists." *Washington Post*. Available at http://www.washingtonpost.com/wp-dyn/content/article/2010/04/28/AR2010042805753.html. Retrieved on September 12, 2012.

5 Braithwaite, T. (2011, March 20). "Dimon warns of bank nail in coffin." *Financial Times*. Available at http://www.ft.com/intl/cms/s/0/3157bcbe-5b05–11e0-a290–00144feab49a.html#axzz1eGrfNk1X. Retrieved on November 20, 2011.

6 Dimon, J. (2012). Annual shareholder's letter. JP Morgan Chase. Available at http://online.wsj.com/public/resources/documents/dimon.pdf. Retrieved on April 5, 2012.

7 Davis Polk. (2010). *Summary of the Dodd-Frank Wall Street reform and consumer protection act, enacted into law on July 21, 2010.* Available

at http://www.davispolk.com/files/publication/7084f9fe-6580–413b-b870-b7c025ed2ecf/presentation/publicationattachment/1d4495c7-0be0-4e9a-ba77-f786fb90464a/070910_financial_reform_summary.pdf. Retrieved on November 20,2011.

8 Mackenzie, M., & Demos, T. (2011, November 13). "Trading reform still years from completion." *Financial Times*. Available at http://www.ft.com/intl/cms/s/0/44d71582–0cb2–11e1–88c6–00144feabdc0.html. Retrieved on November 13, 2011.

9 Board of Governors of the Federal Reserve System. (2008). [Press release]. Available at http://federalreserve.gov/newsevents/press/bcreg/20080921a.htm. Retrieved on November 20, 2011.

10 Johnson, R., & Stiglitz, J. (2012). Letter regarding proposed rule to implement prohibitions and restrictions on proprietary trading and certain interests in, and relationships with, hedge funds and private equity funds. Available at http://www.sec.gov/comments/s7-41-11/s74111-317.pdf. Retrieved on April 4, 2012.

11 Volcker, P. (2012, April 5) "Paul Volcker on the Volcker Rule." [Video interview]. Available at http://billmoyers.com/segment/paul-volcker-on-the-volcker-rule/. Retrieved on April 7, 2012.

12 Lowrey, A. (2012, April 4). "Regulators move closer to oversight of nonbanks." *New York Times*, p. B3.

13 Protess, B. (2011, October 12). "SEC advances Volcker Rule." *New York Times*. Available at http://dealbook.nytimes.com/2011/10/12/s-e-c-advances-volcker-rule/. Retrieved on April 4, 2012.

14 Securities and Exchange Commission. (2012). *Comments on proposed rule: prohibitions and restrictions on proprietary trading and certain interests in, and relationships with, hedge funds and private equity funds.* Available at http://www.sec.gov/comments/s7-41-11/s74111.shtml. Retrieved on April 4, 2012.

15 Stewart, J. (2011, October 21). "Volcker rule, once simple, now boggles." *New York Times*. Available at http://www.nytimes.com/2011/10/22/business/volcker-rule-grows-from-simple-to-complex.html. Retrieved on October 22, 2011.

16 Securities Industry and Financial Markets Association, Asset Management Group. (2012, February 13). Comment letter to SEC: Restrictions on proprietary trading and certain interests in and relationships with hedge funds and private equity funds. Available at http://www.sifma.org/issues/item.aspx?id=8589937354. Retrieved on April 4, 2012.

17 Volcker, P. (2012).

18 Volcker, P. (2012).

19 Anonymous. (2012, February). Private interview by R. Strauss conducted with Wall Street professional.

20 Silver-Greenberg, J., and Schwartz, N. (2012, May 14). "Red flags said to go unheeded by Chase bosses." *New York Times*. Available at http://dealbook.nytimes.com/2012/05/14/warnings-said-to-go-unheeded-by-chase-bosses/?hp. Retrieved on May 14, 2012.

21 Stout, L. A. (2011). "Derivatives and the legal origin of the 2008 credit crisis." *Harvard Business Law Review*, 1(1), pp. 1–38.

22 KPMG. (2010, August 10). "Dodd-Frank Act: Regulation of Over-the-Counter Derivatives". *Regulatory Practice Letter*, (10)13. Available at http://www.kpmg.com/US/en/IssuesAndInsights/ArticlesPublications/regulatory-practice-letters/Documents/rpl-1013-otc-derivatives.pdf. Retrieved on November 9, 2011.

23 Sackheim, M., & Schubert, E. (2011). "Dodd-Frank act has its first birthday, but derivatives end users have little cause to celebrate." *Harvard Business Law Review*. [Online article] Available at http://www.hblr.org/2011/07/derivatives-end-users/. Retrieved on April 6, 2012.

24 KPMG. (2010).

25 European Central Bank. (2011). *The new EU framework for financial crisis management and resolution*, pp. 85–94. Available at http://www.ecb.int/pub/pdf/mobu/mb201107en.pdf. Retrieved on November 22, 2011.

26 Landler, M. (2008, September 30). "The U.S. financial crisis is spreading to Europe." *New York Times*. Available at http://www.nytimes.com/2008/10/01/business/worldbusiness/01global.html. Retrieved on November 24, 2011.

27 British Broadcasting System. (2008, November 3). "Finance crisis: in graphics." *BBC News*. Available at http://news.bbc.co.uk/2/hi/business/7644238.stm. Retrieved on November 23, 2011.

28 Kelly, M. (2010 August). "U.S. bailout funds saved European banks – without much transatlantic reciprocity." Available at http://www.europeaninstitute.org/August-2010/us-bailout-funds-saved-european-banks-without-much-transatlantic-reciprocity.html. Retrieved on November 24, 2011.

29 Bank for International Settlements. (2011). *Fact sheet – Basel Committee on Banking Supervision*. Available at http://www.bis.org/about/factbcbs.htm. Retrieved on November 24, 2011.

30 KPMG. (2011, April 25). "Basel 3, time for banks to engage." *Frontiers in Finance*. Available at http://www.kpmg.com/global/en/issuesandinsights/articlespublications/frontiers-in-finance/publishingimages/frontiersinfinance25april11/april2011/docs/basel_3_apr_2011.pdf. Retrieved on November 23, 2011.

31 Sullivan & Cromwell. (2011). *Basel III Capital and Liquidity Framework*. Available at http://www.sullcrom.com/files/Publication/d6159da8-e931-4b08-bec2-5b3e23dbb035/Presentation/PublicationAttachment/3647a117-0730-4dfd-a8c3-00af96a9f684/SC_Publication_Basel_III_Capital_and_Liquidity_Framework.pdf. Retrieved on April 6, 2012.

32 Ross, C. (2011, June 6). "Basel III: business as usual for bankers." *The Guardian*. Available at http://www.

guardian.co.uk/commentisfree/cifamerica/2011/jun/06/basel-iii-banking-volcker. Retrieved on April 7, 2012.

33 Ross. (2011).

34 Dimon, J. (2012).

35 Harding, R. (2011, August 27). "Lagarde calls for urgent action on banks." *Financial Times.* Available at http://www.ft.com/intl/cms/s/0/9f857244-d0d0–11e0–8891–00144feab49a.html#axzz1edVxHm8l. Retrieved on November 24, 2011.

36 Federal Reserve Bank of the United States (2012, March 13). *Comprehensive Capital Analysis and Review 2012: methodology and results for stress scenario projections.* Available at http://www.federalreserve.gov/newsevents/press/bcreg/bcreg20120313a1.pdf. Retrieved on April 4, 2012.

37 Fitzpatrick, D., & McGrane, V. (2012, March 12). "Stress tests buoy U.S. banks." *Wall Street Journal.* Available at http://online.wsj.com/article/SB10001424052702304537904577279720671471152.html. Retrieved on April 5, 2012.

38 Mattingly, P. (2011, September 13). "FDIC approves 'living wills' for largest bank failures." *Bloomberg.* Available at http://www.bloomberg.com/news/2011–09–13/fdic-to-vote-on-living-wills-for-largest-bank-failures.html. Retrieved on April 5, 2012.

39 Masters, B. (2012, March 4). "Banks drag heels on living wills." *Financial Times.* Available at http://www.ft.com/intl/cms/s/0/44a6a4fc-6391–11e1–9686–00144feabdc0.html#axzz1rBzgMchT. Retrieved on April 4, 2012.

40 Touryalai, H. (2012, March 21). "Volcker rule refugees." *Forbes.* Available at http://www.forbes.com/sites/halahtouryalai/2012/03/21/volcker-rule-refugees/. Retrieved on July 14, 2012.

Chapter Seven   Wall Street Values for the Twenty-First Century

1 McLean, B., & Nocera, J. (2011).
2 Taft, J. G. (2012). *Stewardship: lessons learned from the lost culture of Wall Street*. Hoboken, NJ: John Wiley.
3 Rappeport, A. (2010, April 28). "Blankfein at the Senate hearing into Goldman Sachs." *The Financial Times*. Available at http://blogs.ft.com/businessblog/2010/04/blankfein-at-the-senate-hearing-into-goldman-sachs/. Accessed July 16, 2012.
4 Anonymous. (2011, August). Private interview by R. Strauss conducted with Wall Street professional.
5 Smith, G. (2012, March 14). "Why I Am Leaving Goldman Sachs." *New York Times*. Available at http://www.nytimes.com/2012/03/14/opinion/why-i-am-leaving-goldman-sachs.html?pagewanted=all. Retrieved on July 16, 2012.
6 Goldman Sachs. (2012). "Goldman Sachs' response to March 14, 2012 New York Times Op-ed." Available at http://www.goldmansachs.com/media-relations/comments-and-responses/current/nyt-op-ed-response.html. Retrieved on July 16, 2012.
7 Craig, S. (2012, March 16). "Morgan Stanley Chief told managers not to exploit Goldman's woes." *New York Times*. Available at http://dealbook.nytimes.com/2012/03/16/morgan-stanley-chief-told-managers-not-to-exploit-goldmans-woes/. Retrieved on April 10, 2012.
8 Salmon, F. (2011, October 20). "Is the SEC colluding with banks on CDO prosecutions?" *Reuters*. Available at http://www.reuters.com/article/2011/10/20/idUS399059824020111020. Retrieved on October 22, 2011.
9 Securities and Exchange Commission. (2010). "Goldman Sachs to pay record $550 million to settle SEC charges related to

subprime mortgage CDO." [Press Release] Available at http://www.sec.gov/news/press/2010/2010–123.htm. Retrieved on August, 10, 2011.

10 Bray, C. (2011, October 28). "Judge challenges SEC on Citi settlement." *Wall Street Journal.* Available at http://online.wsj.com/article/SB10001424052970203687504577001880109335126.html?mod=WSJ_hp_LEFTWhatsNewsCollection. Retrieved on October 27, 2011.

11 Office of Inspector General. (2012). Corporate Integrity Agreements. Available at http://oig.hhs.gov/compliance/corporate-integrity-agreements/index.asp. Retrieved on July 16, 2012.

12 Smith. (2012).

13 Goldman Sachs. (2011). *Report of the Business Standard Committee,* p. 20.

14 Allen, K. A. (2011, May). "Prime broker power shift." *Absolute Return Magazine.*

15 JPMorgan Chase. (2011). *Prime brokerage services.* Available at http://www.jpmorgan.com/pages/jpmorgan/investbk/solutions/fixedincome/primebrokerage. Retrieved on November 20, 2011.

16 Craig, S. (2012, April 12). "Goldman fines $22 million over trading huddles." *New York Times.* Available at http://dealbook.nytimes.com/2012/04/12/goldman-fined-22-million-over-trading-huddles/. Retrieved on July 17, 2012.

17 111th Congress of the United States of America. (2010). *Dodd-Frank Wall Street Reform and Consumer Protection Act, Sec. 951. Shareholder vote on executive compensation disclosures.*

18 Kapner, S., Lublin, J. S., & Sidel, R. (2012, April 18). "Citigroup investors reject pay plan." *Wall Street Journal.* Available at http://online.wsj.com/article/SB100014240527023042993045773499312254 59386.html?mod=ITP_pageone_0#articleTabs%3Darticle. Retrieved on April 18, 2012.

19 Ball, D. (2012, February 9). "First for UBS: bonus clawbacks." *Wall Street Journal*. Available at http://online.wsj.com/article/SB10 001424052970204369404577211134184160656.html. Retrieved on April 28, 2012.

20 Zuckerman, G., & Burne, K. (2012, April 6). "'London Whale' rattles debt market." *Wall Street Journal*. Available at http://online. wsj.com/article/SB10001424052702303299604577326031119411 2436.html. Retrieved on May 10, 2012; Eavis, P. (2012, April 6). "What Volcker Rule could mean for JPMorgan's big trades." *New York Times*. Available at http://dealbook.nytimes.com/2012/04/06/ what-volcker-rule-could-mean-for-jpmorgans-big-trades/. Retrieved on July 14, 2012.

21 Dimon, J. (2012).

22 Lau, E. (2012, April 13). "On the Move-Ex-Merrill veterans open independent brokerage firm." *Reuters*. Available at http:// www.reuters.com/article/2012/04/12/snowden-idUSL2E8FCL 0820120412. Retrieved on April 13, 2012.

23 Charles Schwab Corporation. (2012, February 28). "Majority of investment advisors expect an increase in advisors moving to independence, according to Charles Schwab survey." [press release]. Available at http://www.businesswire.com/news/ schwab/20120228005454/en. Retrieved on April 14, 2012.

24 Securities and Exchange Commission. (2011, January 22). "SEC releases staff study recommending a uniform fiduciary standard of conduct for broker-dealers and investment advisers." [Press release]. Available at http://www.sec.gov/news/press/2011/2011–20.htm. Retrieved on April 4, 2011.

25 Mattingly, P., & Hamilton, P. (2012, January 12). "Broker fiduciary rule delayed by cost-benefit analysis, SEC says." *Bloomberg News*. [Press release]. Available at http://www.bloomberg.com/ news/2012-01-12/broker-fiduciary-rule-delayed.html. Retrieved on April 2, 2012.

26 Grind, K., & Ng, S. (2012, April 12). "Blackrock's Street short-cut." *Wall Street Journal.* Available at http://online.wsj.com/article/SB10001424052702303624004577338153082722544.html?mod=dist_smartbrief. Retrieved on April 13, 2012.
27 See Paine, L. S. (2002). *Value shift: why companies must merge social and financial imperatives to achieve superior performance.* New York: McGraw Hill.

Index

Abacus CDOs, 18, 116–117,
    134–136, 145
  SEC and, 18, 135–136
AIG, 9
  bankruptcy of, 110
  TARP and, 79–80
Ameriquest, 8
  subprime mortgage sales
      by, 46
Anderson Mezzanine CDOs,
    133–134

B Corps. *See* Benefit Corporations
Bair, Sheila, 83
banks. *See specific banks*
Bank for International Settlements
    (BIS), 173
Bankers Trust, 104–105
banking industry
  under Basel III proposals,
      173–174
  deregulation of, 73–75
  Glass-Steagall Act, 13, 94
  public confidence in, 10–11

bankruptcy filings
  by AIG, 110
  by Bear Stearns, 110
  by Countrywide, 110
  by Lehman Brothers, 3, 4,
      138–139
  by Wachovia, 110
  by Washington Mutual, 110
Basel Committee on Banking
    Supervision (Basel III),
    173–174
Bear Stearns, 12
  bankruptcy of, 110
  financial bailout of, 85–86
  mortgage-related securities for,
      4, 44
Benefit Corporations (B Corps), 29
Bernanke, Benjamin, 86
The Big Short (Lewis), 83, 119
BIS. *See* Bank for International
    Settlements
Blankfein, Lloyd, 17–18, 179, 181
blue-collar workers, Wall Street as
    influence on, 54–55

Index

bonus compensation packages,
41–43
  clawback policies for, 42–43
  at failed firms, 43, 110–111
  principal transactions and, 41–42
Born, Brooksley, 23, 66, 82, 170
Breeden, Richard, 150
Buffett, Warren, 102, 104
Burry, Mike, 44, 83, 119.
    See also Goldman Sachs
Buttonwood Agreement, 11–12, 92

capital markets, CDOs in, 7
capitalism. *See also* free
    market systems
  Wall Street as threat to, 15–16
Capitalism and Freedom
    (Friedman), 35
CCAR. *See* Comprehensive Capital
    Analysis and Review
CDOs. *See* collateralized debt
    obligations
CDS. *See* credit default swaps
CFMA. *See* Commodity Futures
    Modernization Act
CFTC. *See* Commodities Future
    Trading Commission
Chavez, Alonzo, 56
Churchill, Winston, 61
Citicorp
  SEC settlements against, 137–138
  as TARP recipient, 79
  unloading of toxic assets by,
    136–137
clawback policies, 42–43
client protections
  conflicts of interest with
    preferred clients, 191–193

at Goldman Sachs, lack of,
  123–124
toxic assets and, 136–139
CMOs. *See* collateralized mortgage
  obligations
Cohn, Gary, 181
collateralized debt obligations
  (CDOs), 6. *See also* Abacus CDOs
  Abacus, 18, 116–117, 134–136, 145
  Anderson Mezzanine, 133–134
  in capital markets, 7
  conflict of interest management
    for, 148–149
  development of, 70
  as financial innovation, 7
  at Goldman Sachs, 116, 124–125,
    128–130
  Hudson, 131–132, 144–145
  structural reform for, 146–149
  subprime mortgages and, 6
  Timberwolf, 132–133
collateralized mortgage obligations
  (CMOs), 6–7
  CDOs and, 70
  early development of, 108
  Fannie Mae and, 69–71
  Freddie Mac and, 69–71
  Lehman Brothers and, 109–110
  under SMMEA, 70–71
  subprime mortgages and, 7
  synthetic, 7–8
  Wall Street focus on, 71–73,
    106–113
Commodities Future Trading
  Commission (CFTC), 76
Commodity Futures Modernization
  Act (CFMA) (U.S.), 63, 75–76
  derivatives markets under, 170

Index

compensation packages. *See* bonus
    compensation packages
Comprehensive Capital Analysis
    and Review (CCAR), 175
conflicts of interest
    for CDO management, 148–149
    at Goldman Sachs, 187–188
Congress, U.S., bailouts by, 5
construction industry, Wall Street
    as influence on, 55–56
corporations. *See also* financial
    deregulation era; negligent
    oversight phase; social
    contracts, with corporations
    B Corps, 29
    under free market systems, 33
    Friedman on responsibilities of,
        32, 34, 35, 57, 155–156
    legal rights of, 28
    private, 34
    property rights for, 34
    social responsibility of, 31–36.
        See also Friedman, Milton
    triple bottom line reporting by, 30
counterparties, 17
    for Goldman Sachs, 115
Countrywide, 8
    bankruptcy of, 110
    subprime mortgage sales by, 46
credit default swaps (CDS), 76–80
    in Hudson CDOs, 131

democracy, free market systems
    under, 35
derivatives, 7–8. *See also* synthetic
    CMOs
    under CFMA, 170
    under Dodd-Frank Act, 170–171

Deutsche Bank, 137
Dimon, Jamie, 160, 167–168, 174,
    182. *See also* JPMorgan Chase
    on Volcker Rule, 196
Dodd, Christopher, 157
Dodd-Frank Act (U.S.), 13–14, 156–
    162. *See also* Volcker Rule
    business models influenced by,
        197–200
    complete implementation of,
        161–162
    derivatives market under,
        170–171
    goals of, 157
    SIFMA and, 162
    Wall Street response to, 160–161
Donaldson, Lufkin, and Jenrette, 99
dot-com boom, IPOs and, 126–127

Eisman, Steve, 83, 119, 120.
    See also Goldman Sachs
entrepreneurship, Wall Street's
    influence on, 50–51
    decline during financial crisis,
        50–51
ethics
    with compensation practices,
        193–197
    competition as positive influence
        on, 198–200
    with conflicts of interest, 186–193
    evolution of business models and,
        197–203
    lack of, during financial crisis, 18,
        19, 112–113
    long-term effects of, 19–20
    profitability of, 201–202
    timing factors for, 140–142

Index

Fannie Mae
  CMOs and, 69–71
  establishment of, 68–69
  Ginnie Mae under, 69
  as GSE, 69–71
  MBS and, 46
  subprime mortgages purchased
    by, 8–9
  Wall Street competition with, 109
Federal Home Loan Mortgage
  Corporation. *See* Freddie Mac
Federal Housing Administration
  (FHA), 68–69
Federal National Mortgage
  Association. *See* Fannie Mae
Federal Reserve Bank (U.S.),
  174–175
  CCAR for, 175
FHA. *See* Federal Housing
  Administration
financial crisis, in U.S.
  See also financial deregulation
  era; negligent oversight phase
  avoidability of, 87–88
  as crisis of ethics and values, 19,
    112–113
  Dodd-Frank Act and, 13–14
  forewarnings of, 80–86
  foundations of, 62–63
  mortgage-related securities as
    influence on, 4–5
  new business declines during,
    50–51
  TARP and, 79
Financial Crisis Inquiry
  Commission, 67
financial deregulation era, 64–80
  CDS during, 76–80

commercial banking industry
  during, 73–75
derivative security oversight
  during, 75–80
Financial Crisis Inquiry
  Commission and, 67
Greenspan on, 77–78
investment banking industry
  during, 73–75
mortgage industry transformation
  during, 68–73
original ideology of, 66
Reagan and, 64
financial institutions.
  See also banking industry;
  specific firms
counterparties for, 17
Glass-Steagall Act, 13
global, 12
history of, 11–13
First Franklin, 47
Frank, Barney. *See* Dodd-Frank Act
Freddie Mac
  CMOs and, 69–71
  establishment of, 69
  as GSE, 69–71
  MBS and, 46
  subprime mortgages purchased
    by, 8–9
  Wall Street competition with, 109
free market systems
  under democracy, 35
  efficiency requirements of, 32–33
  freedom of corporations under, 33
  private corporations in, 34
  profit disjunction in, 38–41
  Wall Street as threat to, 15–16,
    36–43

Index

Friedman, Milton, 33, 35
  on libertarian property rights, 34
  on responsibilities of
    corporations, 32, 34, 35, 57,
    155–156

The Gathering Storm (Churchill), 61
Geithner, Timothy, 165
Ginnie Mae, 69
Glass-Steagall Act (U.S.), 13, 63
  repeal of, 73–74, 99–100
  securities industry and, 94,
    99–100
Goldman Sachs, 12
  Abacus CDOs, 18, 116–117,
    134–136, 145
  Anderson Mezzanine CDOs,
    133–134
  CDO investments by, 116,
    128–130
  conflicts of interest at, 187–188
  counterparty losses with, 115
  decline of values at, 125–130
  deliberate market disinformation,
    124–125
  dumping of MBS by, 122–123
  early history of, 93
  Hudson CDOs, 131–132, 144–145
  lack of client protection within,
    123–124
  mortgage-related securities for,
    44
  operating expenses for, 106–107
  organizational strengths of,
    121–122
  prime brokerage services of, 190
  revenues by business segment, 107
  Timberwolf CDOs, 132–133

trading structure for, 128–130
  during 2000s, 105–106
  2007 earnings for, 118–120
Gorman, James, 182
government bailouts. *See* Congress,
  U.S., bailouts by
Government National Mortgage
  Association. *See* Ginnie Mae
government sponsored enterprises
  (GSEs), 69–71. *See also* Fannie
  Mae; Freddie Mac
  Wall Street competition with, 109
Gramm-Leach-Bliley Act (U.S.),
  73–74
  asset risk under, 74
Great Depression, 92–93
The Greatest Trade Ever (Zuckerman),
  83, 119
Greenspan, Alan, 67, 77, 82, 170
  on benefits of financial
    deregulation, 77–78
GSEs. *See* government sponsored
  enterprises
Gutfreund, John, 103–104

housing markets.
  See also mortgage-related
  securities
  Wall Street's influence on, 15,
    43–47
Hubler, Howie, 18
Hudson CDOs, 131–132, 144–145
  CDS in, 131
  RBMS and, 131

Iksil, Bruno, 194
IMF. *See* International Monetary
  Fund

Index

initial public offerings (IPOs),
126–127
International Monetary Fund
(IMF), 172–173
investment banking industry,
deregulation of, 73–75
Citicorp and, 74
expansion of leverage ratios for,
74–75
Investment Company Act (U.S.),
199
IPOs. *See* initial public offerings

Johnson, Robert, 164
JPMorgan Chase, 12
as prime brokerage service, 190
SEC settlements against, 137–138
unloading of toxic assets by,
136–137

labor markets, Wall Street as
influence on, 53–57
construction industry, 55–56
faulty signaling to blue-collar
workers, 54–55
unemployment duration and,
53–54
Lagarde, Christine, 174
Lehman Brothers, 12
bankruptcy filing by, 3, 4, 110,
138–139
CMOs and, 109–110
mortgage-related securities for, 44
unloading of toxic assets by,
138–139
leverage ratios, expansion of, 74–75
Levin, Carl, 117, 180
Levitt, Arthur, 77, 170

Lewis, Michael, 83, 119
Long Term Capital Management,
bailout of, 76

market-making, proprietary trading
compared to, 196–197
Marquez, Valentin, 55
Marrero, Victor, 145
Mayer, Martin, 94–95
MBS. *See* mortgage-backed
securities
Merrill, Charles E., 94–95, 198
Merrill Lynch, 12
business model of, 95–96
claims settlements against, 105
First Franklin purchased by, 47
mortgage-related securities for,
4, 44
Mitchell, Charles E., 93
Moodys, subprime mortgage ratings
for, 8
Mooney, Robert, 199
moral hazards, 180–186,
definition of, 184
moral, 185
Morgan Stanley, 18, 144, 146,
164, 190
mortgage industry.
See also collateralized mortgage
obligations; Fannie Mae;
Freddie Mac; mortgage-related
securities; subprime mortgages
FHA and, 68–69
during financial deregulation era,
68–73
under New Deal, 68
non-agency loans, 71
under SMMEA, 70–71

Index

mortgage-backed securities (MBS), 45–47
  Fannie Mae and, 46
  Freddie Mac and, 46
  Goldman Sachs' dumping of, 122–123
mortgage-related securities
  for Bear Stearns, 4, 44
  congressional bailout for, 5
  global financial crisis and, 4–5
  for Goldman Sachs, 44
  for Lehman Brothers, 44
  MBS, 45–47
  for Merrill Lynch, 4, 44
  Wall Street focus on, 43–47
Moser, Paul, 103

negligent oversight phase, 80–86
  forewarnings of financial crisis during, 85–86
New Century, subprime mortgage sales by, 46
New Deal. *See* Roosevelt, Franklin Delano
New York Stock Exchange (NYSE)
  Buttonwood Agreement and, 11–12, 92
  early partnership rules of, 97–98
  1929 Stock Crash, 92–93
  securities industry reform after, 93–95
non-agency mortgage loans, 71
NYSE. *See* New York Stock Exchange

Obama, Barack, 156
Occupy Wall Street movement, 10–11

On the Brink (Paulson, H.), 89
O'Neal, Stanley, 36–37, 122

Pandit, Vikram, 89
Paulson, Henry, 36, 81, 84, 89
Paulson, John, 44, 83, 119, 120, 131, 143. *See also* Goldman Sachs
Phillips, Susan, 72–73
Primary Reserve Fund, 3–4
principal transactions, 41–42
private corporations, 34
profit disjunction, 38–41
property rights, for corporations, 34
proprietary trading, under Volcker Rule, 163, 166–167
  asset-liability management compared to, 194–195
  market-making compared to, 196–197

Rajan, Raghuran G., 81
Rakoff, Jed, 183
Ranieri, Lewis, 70, 108
rating agencies. *See* Moodys, subprime mortgage ratings for; Standard and Poors, subprime mortgage ratings for
RBMS. *See* Residential Mortgage-backed Securities
Reagan, Ronald, 64
Residential Mortgage-backed Securities (RBMS), 131
  Deutsche Bank and, 137
Roosevelt, Franklin Delano, 68
Rubin, Robert, 67, 77, 82, 84, 170

Index

Salomon Brothers, 102
  Buffett and, 102, 104
  decline of, 102–104
  income statement for
    (1986–1990), 103–106
SEC. *See* Securities and Exchange
  Commission
Secondary Mortgage Market
  Enhancement Act (SMMEA)
  (U.S.), 70–71
Securities and Exchange
  Commission (SEC)
  Abacus case and, 18, 135–136
  Citicorp settlements with,
    137–138
  early development of,
    93–94
  JPMorgan Chase settlements
    with, 137–138
securities industry. *See also*
  Dodd-Frank Act;
  mortgage-related securities;
  Volcker, Paul; *specific firms*
  Buttonwood Agreement and,
    11–12, 92
  changes in traditional business
    models, 100–101
  development history of, 92–97
  expansion of, 99–100
  Glass-Steagall Act and, 94,
    99–100
  during 1980s, 102
  during 1990s, 102–105
  public investment after 1970,
    98–100
  reform after 1929 Stock Crash,
    93–95
  during 2000s, 105–106

Security Industry Financial
  Management Association
  (SIFMA), 162
Shapiro, Mary, 200
Shelby, Richard, 157
SIFMA. *See* Security Industry
  Financial Management
  Association
Smith, Adam, 32, 33
Smith, Greg, 180, 185
SMMEA. *See* Secondary Mortgage
  Market Enhancement Act
social contracts, with corporations,
  27–31
  B Corps in, 29
  legal rights within, 28
  minimalist view for, 31–36.
    See also Friedman, Milton
  social obligations under, 28–29
  triple bottom line reporting as
    part of, 30
  United Nations Global Compact,
    30, 206
Standard and Poors, subprime
  mortgage ratings for, 8
Stein, Sidney, 147
Stewart, James B., 166
Stiglitz, Joseph, 164
subprime mortgages
  Ameriquest sales of, 46
  CDOs and, 6
  CMOs and, 7
  Fannie Mae purchases of, 8–9
  Freddie Mac purchases of, 8–9
  New Century sales of, 46
  ratings for, 8
Summers, Larry, 67, 77, 82
Swenson, Michael, 121

Index

synthetic CMOs, 7–8

Taft, Robert, 180
TARP. *See* Troubled Assets Relief
 Program
Timberwolf CDOs, 132–133
too big to fail, Wall Street as, 6
Tourre, Fabrice, 145
trading. *See* proprietary trading,
 under Volcker Rule
triple bottom line reporting, 30
Troubled Assets Relief Program
 (TARP), 79, 88
 AIG and, 79–80
Turyalai, Hala, 176

unemployment, duration of, 53–54
United Nations Global Compact, 30
 principles of, 206
United States (U.S.).
 See also Dodd-Frank Act;
 financial crisis, in U.S.;
 financial deregulation era;
 Glass-Steagall Act; negligent
 oversight phase
 CFMA in, 63, 75–76
 congressional bailouts of Wall
  Street, 5
 Federal Reserve Bank in, 174–175
 Gramm-Leach-Bliley Act in,
  73–74
 Great Depression in, 92–93
 Investment Company Act in, 199
 1929 Stock Crash in, 92–93
 SMMEA in, 70–71
 Wall Street prosperity compared
  to national financial
  welfare, 13

values, 19. *See also* ethics
 with compensation practices,
  193–197
 competition as positive influence
  on, 198–200
 with conflicts of interest, 186–193
 decline of, at Goldman Sachs,
  125–130
 evolution of business models and,
  197–203
 lack of, during financial crisis, 19,
  112–113
 long-term effects of, 19–20
 moral hazards, 180–186,
 profitability of, 201–202
 sustainability of, 150–152
 timing factors for, 140–142
Valukas, Anton R., 139
Viniar, David, 120
Volcker, Paul, 155, 167
 Dimon on, 167–168
Volcker Rule, 163–170
 Dimon on, 196
 proprietary trading under, 163,
  166–167, 194–195, 196–197
 purpose of, 164

Wachovia, bankruptcy filing
 by, 110
Wall Street. *See also* Dodd-Frank
 Act; ethics; financial
 deregulation era; Glass-Steagall
 Act; negligent oversight phase;
 securities industry; social
 contracts, with corporations;
 values
 blue-collar workers influenced by,
  54–55